v

To begin with . . .

With the steady increase in foreign travel, more and more of us go each year for the first time to the Rhineland or to Austria, or enjoy a winter-sports holiday in Switzerland. But very few feel confident enough to try out their text-book German in a shop or at the railway station. A party often tends to rely on one spokesman, and it is usually a relief to find that the shop-keepers speak English!

There are two good reasons why beginners find it difficult to "launch out" in German. First there are the "endings"; the shop is der Laden, but you go into den Laden and once inside you are in dem Laden, which is all very confusing. Then we have the word-order; there is a popular but mistaken idea that German sentences are spoken and written backwards!

One aim of this book is to simplify the learning of endings. You will find them occurring naturally in things you will want to say, arranged in the order in which you yourself will need them, and not in the rather forbidding tables of the traditional grammar book. The gradual lengthening of the sentences along natural lines will build up without strain all you require in the way of word-order.

This is the simplest and the most informal of the German books in the "Teach Yourself" series. It is designed with the younger reader in mind who might wish to supplement or replace a school primer and also those adults who, from scratch, would like to acquire a quick and accurate knowledge of basic everyday German. The vocabulary is based on common interests, and if the word lists are learned systematically they will soon provide a useful stock of German words for most everyday occasions.

Part II contains the answers to the Exercises in Part I. They should not, of course, be referred to before the exercises have been worked through. Much can be gained by trying to locate where you have gone wrong if the answer in the Key differs from your own version. It is also important to work at the speed which suits you best. Complete confidence at each stage is the secret of language learning, and it is not a sign of weakness to go back to an earlier Lesson whenever a point is not quite clear.

Each Lesson ends with a "Have a Try" section which purposely introduces a few new words and constructions in advance of the text. These passages are intended as a challenge and sometimes as an entertainment. They offer an opportunity for intelligent deduction if the temptation to look up new words is resisted; the general sense provides adequate clues to their meaning.

So much by way of introduction; now we are ready to get to grips with Lesson I. "Frisch gewagt ist halb gewonnen", as the Germans say.

How to Pronounce German

Can you imitate a Welshman's way of speaking, or an Irishman's—or put on a Birmingham "accent"? If you can, you find yourself changing your usual emphasis, speed and tone of voice, besides producing some of the sounds differently.

Very little of this can be explained on paper. So it is with a foreign language: the only way to pronounce German correctly is to imitate a German-speaking person or a very good teacher. The radio and records or tapes are good substitutes—but you must practise hard and often, say for twenty minutes at a time, and it's easier if you have a talent for mimicry.

To read and write German, you have of course to be able to associate the sounds with the actual letters of the alphabet that represent them. For reference, here are a few hints about some of the "catches". They will help you to link up what you hear with the written and printed words.

Before you read on, notice that this section is not a "Lesson" to be worked through. Refer to it all the time you are learning until your spelling and pronunciation go hand in hand. It is not a complete treatise on pronunciation, but it will give you all the practical help you need.

Consonants

Five are particularly likely to catch you out:

Z sounds like TS (*Z*immer)
J sounds like Y (*J*a, *J*unge)
W sounds like V (*W*inter, *w*as)
V sounds like F (*V*ater, *v*on)
S sounds like Z (*s*ehen, *s*o)
[except at the
end of a word,
when it is like s
in English] (Hau*s*, e*s*)

Then you must be careful about *SCH* and *CH*:

In *SCH* the *C* is silent. Imagine you are telling someone to be quiet—SH!—but keep your teeth together.

SCH comes before all consonants except P and T (Sch*l*ange, Sch*r*aube, Sch*n*itt, sch*m*al, etc.).

But even SP and ST (e.g. *sp*rechen, *st*ehen) sound as though the CH was still there (that is, like schprechen, schtehen).

(*N.B.*—NEVER write *SH* in German!)

CH after i, e, ü, ö and ä (i*ch*, fre*ch*, Bü*ch*er, Mön*ch*, lä*ch*eln) is pronounced by trying to say *SCH* without letting the teeth meet.

But *CH* after a, o, u, au (Ba*ch*, po*ch*en, Bu*ch*, au*ch*) sounds like the ch in Scottish "loch".

Notice also the following:

Final D and *B* sound like T and P (Hun*d*, blie*b*). (Think how you say "walke*d*" in English.)

K   replaces the English C in *k*ann, *K*atze, etc.

H   is heard except after vowels (se*h*en, ne*h*men) where it merely lengthens the vowel.

R   must be pronounced, especially in words such as Mutte*r*. It is not necessarily a "uvular r" as in French. Always pronounce initial R without using the lips—don't pronounce *r*echt as though it was oo-recht.

G   is hard in almost every case, but *NG* is soft as in "bring".

L   is pronounced without curling up the tongue: let it touch your teeth.

QU is pronounced *KV*.

Vowels

U   sounds like the "oo" in English "fool".

A is pronounced with the tongue flat and the mouth opened "square".

AU sounds rather like "ow" in English "now".

EU is like the "oy" in "boy".

AI and *EI* are like the "i" in "mind".

IE sounds like the "ee" in "teeth".

OO is just a long O: thus "Boot" rhymes (approximately with "coat", not "coot".

EE is similarly a long E: thus "Beet" rhymes (approximately) with "fate" and not with "feet".

A vowel followed by a doubled consonant is normally *short*:

Mann, voll, Henne,

but one followed by a single consonant or h + consonant is *long*:

Tal, fehlt.

German words have no accents, cedillas, etc., and no nasal sounds. There are no words like English "cough", "bough" and "night" and no radically different ways of pronouncing the same letter.

Notice however the Umlaut (written ··). It is really a letter "e" and is added only to "a", "o" and "u".

> ä sounds like German "e"
> ö sounds like "eu" in French
> ü sounds like "ee" said with rounded lips
> äu sounds like German "eu"

PART I

LESSON ONE

HOW TO SAY "THE" AND "A", "THIS" AND "THAT"

Where shall we begin? The best way is to learn the names of a few things and persons in German and make simple sentences out of them. Such words are called nouns, and they are easy to recognise in German because they *all* begin with a capital letter.

The only difficulty at this stage is the existence of three words, *der*, *die* and *das*, all meaning the same thing: "*the*". This, the grammar books tell us, is due to the fact that nouns are of three different types or genders, as they put it—but don't let this worry you.

Grammatical "gender" depends much more on the origin and spelling of nouns than on their meaning. Thus all words ending in -chen and -lein have das, most nouns ending in -e and all those ending in -heit, -keit, -ung and -in have die, and most of those ending in -er have der. This explains why all nouns, things as well as persons, can be "masculine" (der), "feminine" (die) or "neuter" (das). The names of most *persons* whom we think of as masculine or feminine—"father", "footballer", "nurse", "queen", for example—are in fact der or die words, but the *things* are fairly evenly distributed between der, die and das.

So the best method is to learn each noun as you come to it simply as a *der*, *die or das word*. Always learn the word for "the" along with the noun; thus—"the book" = *das* Buch. This plan will also cover those nouns whose "gender" cannot be told from their spelling.

You would soon get tired of using only "the" with nouns, so let us learn the German for "a" (or "an") as well:

ein = "a" with der and das words
eine = "a" with die words

I

Here are some other substitutes for der, die and das which will make your sentences more interesting:

dieser,	diese,	dieses	this
jener,	jene,	jenes	that (English "yon")
jeder,	jede,	jedes	every
welcher,	welche,	welches	which?

(Note that the -e of these words replaces the -ie of die and the -es replaces the -as of das. Dieser, jener, etc. obviously replace der.)

Adjectives

Words such as "big", "old" and "white", which tell us what a person or thing is like, are called adjectives. In this Lesson we will learn some to put along with our nouns. This is very easy to do in German, because adjectives do not have to "agree" with their nouns as they do in French.

So we can say:

> Der Grossvater ist *alt*
> Die Grossmutter ist *alt*
> Das Haus ist *alt*

The word alt ("old") can describe nouns of all three types without changing its spelling—exactly like its English equivalent.

There are just two things we must not try to do for the present: we must not try to make nouns *plural*, and although we can say "The bread is white" we must not attempt to say "white bread", i.e. to put adjectives *in front* of nouns. You will soon see why!

Now let us learn the words in the following list and see how they work in our first exercises:

Word List 1

der Ball, the ball
der Hund, the dog
der Junge, the boy
der Laden, the shop

der Sohn, the son
der Vater (Grossvater), the father (grandfather)
die Brille, the (pair of) spectacles

die Familie, the family
die Mutter (Grossmutter), the mother (grandmother)
die Pfeife, the pipe
die Puppe, the doll
die Strasse, the street
die Tür, the door
die Zeitung, the newspaper
das Brot, the bread
das Haus, the house
das Mädchen, the girl
das Zimmer, the room
alt, old
breit, wide
hell, bright
hübsch, pretty
jung, young
klein, little
offen, open

rund, round
weiss, white
bellt, barks
hat, has
holt, fetches
ist, is
ruft, calls
spielt, plays
sucht, looks for
wohnt, lives
was? what?
wer? who?
wie? what is . . . like?
aber, but
hier, here
laut, loud(ly)
und, and
wo? where?

Exercise 1 (*a*)

Put into English:

1. Die Mutter holt das Brot. 2. Đer Grossvater hat eine Brille und eine Zeitung. 3. Das Mädchen hat eine Puppe. Die Puppe ist hübsch. 4. Dieser Ball ist rund. 5. Dieses Haus ist klein, aber die Strasse ist breit. 6. Die Familie wohnt hier. 7. Jener Laden ist offen. 8. Wer ist Karl? Karl ist der Sohn. Karl ist ein Junge. 9. Wie ist der Hund? Der Hund ist weiss. 10. Jeder Sohn ist ein Junge. 11. Der Grossvater hat eine Pfeife.

Exercise 1 (*b*)

Complete:

1. Dies— Zim—— — h——. 2. Jen— H—— s—— Karl. 3. Dies— Lad— — kl——. 4. D— Mut—— r—— d— Mäd——. 5. Ei— Junge sp—— h——.

Put into German:

6. That dog fetches a newspaper. 7. The dog barks loudly. 8. What is this bread like? 9. Where is that ball? 10. A room has a door. 11. Is every girl pretty? 12. Who lives here?

Have a Try 1

Helga bringt ihre Puppe in das Zimmer. Der Grossvater sucht seine Brille überall. Ohne Brille kann er die Zeitung nicht lesen. Er raucht eine Pfeife. Hier liegt der Hund, und dort ist ein Ball. Der Junge spielt oft mit dem Ball in dem Garten. Was macht die Mutter? Sie holt das Brot, und die Familie kommt in das Esszimmer. Das Mittagessen riecht gut, und sie essen alle mit gutem Appetit!

LESSON TWO

HOW TO SAY "I AM PLAYING" AND "I AM NOT PLAYING". HOW TO ASK QUESTIONS

In order to make the sentences in Lesson One we already had to use words such as spielt and wohnt. These words, which tell us what people do, are *verbs*. Spielt, remember, means "plays": we can say Karl spielt or Der Hund spielt, but obviously not "I plays" and "we, you or they plays". Now let us see how these other persons are dealt with.

Here are the persons:

I,	ich	we,	wir
he,	er	you,	*S*ie
she,	sie	they,	sie

Be careful with "it". "It" = *er* (referring to a der word), *sie* (referring to a die word) or *es* (referring to a das word).

Er can mean "he" or "it" because we might be talking about a der person or a der thing: sie can mean "she", "it" or "they".

There is also a person du (compare "thou" in English and "tu" in French). It is used only when talking to animals or small children, by children talking to one another, or by adults when they address members of their own family or very old friends. We had better know it, but never use it to a stranger when you are abroad. Sie will be your word for "you", whether you are speaking to one person or to several.

Now for some verbs.

We already know that "he, she or it plays" will be er, sie, es } spielt

Learn next   I play = ich spiel*e*
                     and

we, you, they } play = wir, Sie, sie } spiel*en*

5

Here is a piece of luck. As in English, the same word goes with all three persons.

(With du the ending would be -st: du spiel*st*. Compare this with the English "thou ha*st*".)

Let us sum up what we have just been doing. In English, verbs with "he", "she" and "it" end in -s: in German this is replaced by a -t. In addition, German verbs with ich have a special ending -e, and with "we", "you" and "they" they need -en.

The grammar books call this making the Present Tense of a verb. It is really very easy, and here is the best thing about it: not only spiel- but practically all German verbs are treated like this, except two or three that we shall see later. (They are easier still!)

So "I go" will be ich geh*e*, "we find"—wir find*en*, "he writes"—er schreib*t*, and so on.

Before we go on, there is just one small problem to clear up. If you look up a verb in a dictionary, you will find there is no room for all the different persons, and all that appears is: gehen = "to go", trinken = "to drink", kommen = "to come", etc. Except in the case of a few verbs such as wandern —"to wander" and lächeln—"to smile", which you can consider as shortened forms of wanderen and lächelen, the "dictionary form" of the verb in German always ends in -EN. Its technical name is the Infinitive—the "unfinished" form of the verb which it is our job to finish, by taking off the -EN and putting on the endings to match the various persons. In most languages infinitives and persons can have several alternative endings; in German we are spared this complication. Notice too how convenient it is that the infinitive and all the persons "we", "you" and "they" share the same ending -en.

How to ask questions

First a word about the meaning of what we have just been learning. It is important to know that ich spiele means "I am playing" and "I do play" as well as just "I play". Er wohnt can be "he is living", and so on.

This is very useful when we want to ask questions.

> "Do you live here?" simply becomes Wohnen Sie hier?
> "Is he playing?" becomes Spielt er?

This works with nouns too. "Does the dog play?" is Spielt der Hund?

Never bring in "is", "do" and "does" in a German question; just turn round the verb and its noun or pronoun. We often do this in English, of course; just consider "Have you?" or "How goes the battle?" In German, do it *every time*.

Questions such as "Who is . . . ?", "Where are . . . ?" are just the same in German: Wer ist alt?, Wo ist das Brot?

How to say "I am not playing"

Simply put *nicht* after the verb—ich spiele nicht—(never between the person and the verb).

So "he doesn't live" is er wohnt nicht, "we are not going" is wir gehen nicht, and so on. Sometimes a few words come before the nicht is put in; "I don't fetch the wood" would be ich hole das Holz nicht.

When the sentence ends with an *adjective*, put the nicht in front of this. "The doll is not pretty" is Die Puppe ist *nicht hübsch*. Think of a man being alt or nicht alt, a thing as rund or nicht rund, etc.

One other point: nicht ein and nicht eine become *kein* and *keine*. So "I haven't a car" (or "I have no car") is ich habe *kein* Auto.

Now for our second word list, and some exercises in which to practise all this.

Word List 2

der Apfel, the apple	der Himmel, the sky
der Bahnhof, the station	der Nachbar, the neighbour
der Freund, the friend	der Onkel, the uncle
der Garten, the garden	der Tischler, the joiner

der Vogel, the bird
die Apfelsine, the orange
die Jacke, the (sports) coat
die Post, the post office
die Tante, the aunt
das Auto, the car
das Hotel, the hotel
das Klavier, the piano
das Spielzeug, the toy
bitte, please
ja, yes
nein, no
gelb, yellow
grün, green
blau, blue
gross, big
dort, there

nebenan, next door
sehr, very
angeln, to fish
beissen, to bite
fliegen, to fly
gehen, to go
hämmern, to hammer
kommen, to come
lernen, to learn
rauchen, to smoke
schreiben, to write
schwimmen, to swim
singen, to sing
stehen, to stand
stricken, to knit
tanzen, to dance

Exercise 2 (*a*)

Practise these nouns aloud and in writing with all the verbs in the List that fit. The first two are done for you:

der Vater	raucht : singt nicht
die Mutter	strickt : angelt nicht
der Freund	
ein Mädchen	
die Tante	
dieser Junge	
der Onkel	
ein Tischler	
der Nachbar	
ein Vogel	

Now try them as questions: Raucht der Vater? etc.

Exercise 2 (*b*)

Put into English:

1. Bitte, wo ist der Bahnhof? 2. Spielen Sie (das) Klavier? 3. Dieser Junge hat kein Spielzeug. 4. Wohnen der Onkel und die Tante nebenan? 5. Fliegt ein Hund? Nein, er fliegt nicht.

Answer in German:

6. Strickt der Grossvater? 7. Wie ist das Hotel? 8. Haben Sie ein Auto?

Write the *questions* which would receive the following answers:

9. Nein, eine Apfelsine ist gelb. 10. Ja, die Grossmutter strickt. 11. Dort steht der Onkel. 12. Er ist blau.

Exercise 2 (c)

Put into German:

1. Does this dog bite? No, he doesn't bite. 2. Are you wearing a coat? 3. This garden is not very big. 4. Is that girl dancing? 5. Are you looking for the post office? 6. This apple isn't green. 7. Where is the hotel? 8. Is that bird yellow? 9. No, we don't sing. 10. Is a boy playing the piano next door?

Have a Try 2

Ein Auto steht vor der Post, und unser Nachbar steigt aus. Warum (why) geht er in das Postamt? Er hat keine Briefmarken und muss einen Brief auf die Post geben. Ein Junge kommt in die Strasse, wo mein Onkel wohnt, und geht zur Tür seines Hauses. Der Hund bellt nicht, denn (for) er kennt Karl. Meine Tante gibt ihm eine Apfelsine.

Nebenan arbeitet ein Mann im Garten, denn der Himmel ist blau und es regnet nicht.

HOW TO SAY "MY" AND "HIS". HOW TO TELL PEOPLE WHAT TO DO. MORE ABOUT VERBS. A NEW "ENDING"

"My", "his", etc.

Here are some more useful words to replace "the" and "a". You will have noticed two of them in the last "Have a Try" piece.

(followed by a der or das word)	(followed by a die word)
my = mein	meine
his = sein	seine
her = ihr	ihre
its = sein (or ihr if the possessor is a die word)	seine (or ihre)
our = unser	unsere
your = Ihr	Ihre
their = ihr	ihre

(with du, the word for "your" would be dein(e))

Mein and sein will obviously work exactly like ein; although the other words in this list don't rhyme with them, they are used in just the same way.

Commands

Speak!—Sprechen Sie!   Look for it!—Suchen Sie es!

All you have to do is to put in the extra Sie after the verb, which of course ends in -en. Don't forget the exclamation mark, otherwise these commands would look like questions. "Don't speak!" is simply Sprechen Sie *nicht*!

More about verbs

A few verbs have a little "catch" when used with er, sie or es. (There are no irregularities with ich or in the plural.)

Learn the following:

ich	*wir, Sie, sie*		BUT *er, sie, es*
gebe	geben	(give)	g*i*bt
helfe	helfen	(help)	h*i*lft
lese	lesen	(read)	l*ie*st
nehme	nehmen	(take)	n*imm*t
sehe	sehen	(see)	s*ie*ht
spreche	sprechen	(speak)	spr*i*cht
treffe	treffen	(meet)	tr*i*fft
werfe	werfen	(throw)	w*i*rft

(This does not happen with gehen and stehen: er geht, steht)

fahre	fahren	(go)	f*ä*hrt
falle	fallen	(fall)	f*ä*llt
halte	halten	(hold)	h*ä*lt
laufe	laufen	(run)	l*äu*ft
schlafe	schlafen	(sleep)	schl*ä*ft
schlage	schlagen	(hit)	schl*ä*gt
trage	tragen	(carry, wear)	tr*ä*gt

The catch is that "e" becomes "i" (occasionally "ie"), and "a" becomes "ä"—only with er, sie, es (and du).

(The change to "ä" does not occur in macht, sagt, fragt, jagt.)

Notice also what is done with finden and öffnen (to open). As it would be impossible to pronounce er, sie, es find*t* or öff*n*t, we must say find*e*t and öffn*e*t. This extra "e" is needed only when a "t" (i.e. the ending with er, sie or es) has to follow "*n*" or "*d*". It is not necessary in schliesst, sitzt, hebt etc.

"To be" and "to have"

The verb "to be" is very easy in German. We already know that "is" = ist. Just learn in addition that ich BIN = "I am" and wir, Sie, sie SIND = "we, you and they are".

Finally, there is one trap in the verb "to have". Ich habe and wir, Sie, sie haben are just what we would expect. But "has" is HAT; the "b" drops out just as the "v" does in the English equivalent.

A New Ending

Just look at these sentences:

> Die Mutter holt das Brot
> Der Grossvater nimmt seine Brille
> Der Hund jagt *den* Ball

In the last one den has replaced der. To understand why, think how these sentences are built. Because someone fetches the bread, picks up the glasses and chases the ball, each of these nouns is called the *object* of the verb, just as the mother, dog, etc., who do the fetching and chasing, are called the *subject*. When you sharpen a pencil, buy a suit or clean your shoes, all these things are "objects".

In English this is simply a grammatical idea: the spelling and appearance of the words are not affected at all. In German there is very little difference either, except in one vital case: when the object happens to be a der word. Then DER becomes DEN, and any other word taking the place of "the" must likewise end in -EN.

So we must say:

> Der Hund jagt d*en* (ein*en*, dies*en*, sein*en*, etc.) Ball.

This is the first of the troublesome endings we mentioned at the beginning of this book. Try to recognise when you make a noun the object in a sentence. If it is a der word, then *any* word in front of it will end in -EN. You can practise this in the exercises below.

Word List 3

der Bleistift, the pencil	der Kugelschreiber, the ball-point pen
der Brief, the letter	der Schlüssel, the key
der Bruder, the brother	der Schnee, the snow
der Eimer, the bucket	der Tau, the dew
der Gärtner, the gardener	der Teller, the plate
der Farbstift, the crayon	die Füllfeder, the fountain pen
der Kellner, the waiter	die Mauer, the wall
der Krug, the jug	die Putzfrau, the charlady

die Schubkarre, the wheelbarrow
die Schwester, the sister
das Lineal, the ruler
das Löschblatt, the blotting-paper
das Taschenmesser, the penknife
das Trinkglas, the tumbler
bringen, to bring
fahren, to go (by vehicle)
fallen, to fall
finden, to find
halten, to hold
jagen, to chase
kaufen, to buy
leeren, to empty

lesen, to read
nehmen, to take
pflegen, to look after
sehen, to see
schlafen, to sleep
tragen, to carry, wear
treffen, to meet
werfen, to throw
zeigen, to show
zerbrechen, to break
kalt, cold
über, over

Exercise 3 (*a*)

Complete the following sentences by putting the correct words in columns two and three:

ich	(halten)	mei—	Schlüssel
Karl	(nehmen)	sei—	Kugelschreiber
Grete	(suchen)	ihr—	Farbstift
wir	(pflegen)	uns—	Garten
Sie	(finden)	Ih—	Lineal
sie	(sehen)	ih—	Bruder
dieser Junge	(treffen)	sei—	Schwester

Now try them with other verbs and nouns in columns two and four:

e.g. Karl *liest* seinen *Brief*

Exercise 3 (*b*)

Put into German:

1. Fetch your glass! 2. Has the gardener his wheelbarrow? 3. The charlady empties her bucket. 4. Don't break that jug! 5. Have you my ruler? 6. Inge takes her pen and writes a letter. 7. Give me (mir) your penknife. 8. My sister isn't carrying her doll. 9. Has your father his key? 10. The waiter brings me a plate. 11. It is cold; the dew is falling. 12. Show me your sportscoat.

Exercise 3 (c)

Complete:

1. N—— dies— Junge s—— Taschenmesser? 2. Mei—
Vater l—— sei—— Brief. 3. W—rf— Ih— Bruder
sei—— Ball? 4. Lee—— —— dies— Trinkglas! 5.
Uns—— Putzfrau h— ih—— Eimer.

Put into English:

6. Zerbrechen Sie nicht meinen Kugelschreiber! 7. Jagt der
Gärtner jenen Hund? 8. Holen Sie einen Apfel und einen
Teller! 9. Hans wirft seinen Ball über die Mauer. 10. Haben
Sie einen Bruder oder eine Schwester?

Have a Try 3

Ein Gärtner arbeitet im Park. Er gräbt die Blumenbeete
um und schiebt seine Schubkarre den Pfad entlang. Die Rosen
blühen im hellen Sonnenschein. Ein Vogel setzt sich (perches)
auf die Schubkarre, denn er sieht einen dicken Wurm. Der
Gärtner muss die Blumen am Abend begiessen (water), wenn
es nicht regnet. Das Gras ist kurz, denn er hat einen guten
Rasenmäher.

MORE ABOUT ADJECTIVES. SOME REVISION EXERCISES

The most useful thing to learn next is how to put adjectives in front of nouns. In a shop you would want to buy not just a pen or a shirt, but more likely a *good* pen or a *white* shirt. Let us see how this is done.

a good pen = eine gut*e* Feder; a white shirt = ein weiss*es* Hemd

Now look at these other examples:

kaltes Wasser: ein brauner Vogel; mein neues Buch; dicker Schnee; dieser rote Apfel; das grosse Hotel; der blaue Himmel; ihr leerer Eimer; ich sehe einen grünen Farbstift, meinen alten Freund, jenen langen Brief

First, adjectives *do* come before the noun, never after it, as so often happens in French (e.g. "le Moulin Rouge").

Next, when they do so, they *must* have an ending. But there are only four endings to choose from, -E, -ER or -ES, and -EN. Can you see when each of these is needed?

If the first word has no ending (ein, mein, ihr, etc.) or if there is no word there at all (cold water, red ink, etc.), then the adjective has -ER with der words and -ES with das words. This is really a help, as the ending shows the gender. (Standing alone before a die word, adjectives have -E.)

If the first word already shows the gender (der, die, das, dieser, eine, etc.), then nothing special is needed, and all the adjectives have a "neutral" -E.

If the first word has been changed (so far this happens only with der words used as objects, when the first word becomes den, einen, etc.), then the adjective has -EN.

This is not so difficult after all, though we have here a very important group of "endings". You can try them out for yourself below.

As the previous Lessons contain quite a lot to remember, the exercises in this Lesson give you some more practice in the things we have done so far.

Word List 4

der Dackel, dachshund
der Gasherd, the gas-cooker
der Kleiderschrank, the wardrobe
der Kühlschrank, the refrigerator
der Spülstein, the sink
der Stuhl, the chair
der Teppich, the carpet
der Tisch, the table
der Wecker, the alarm-clock
die Blumenvase, the flower-vase
die Küche, the kitchen
die Küchenuhr, the kitchen clock
die Tasche, the pocket
das Bett, the bed
das Bild, the picture
das Büfett, the sideboard
das Feuer, the fire
das Radio, the radio
das Taschentuch, the handkerchief
das Wasser, the water

die Uhr can also mean "the watch"

bequem, comfortable
bunt, coloured
elektrisch, electric
frisch, new, fresh
hoch, tall, high (hoh-e, etc.)
kaputt, broken
lang, long
neu, new
praktisch, useful, practical
rein, clean
rostig, rusty
saftig, juicy
schmutzig, dirty
schön, fine, beautiful
tief, deep
weich, soft
zuverlässig, reliable
heute morgen, this morning
lange, a long time
ich möchte, I would like (to)
ach!, oh! oh dear!
rasseln, to rattle, ring (of an alarm clock)

Exercise 4 (a)

In the kitchen	In the bedroom	In the living-room
ein neuer Gasherd der ——— ———	mein bequemes Bett dies——— ——— ———	ein runder Tisch unser ——— ———

Continue these tables by placing each of the following things in the correct room. Put the most suitable adjective from the given list with each one, and vary the first words as shown in the examples:

der Wecker, das Büfett, der Kleiderschrank, die Küchenuhr, das Bild, der Teppich, der Spülstein, die Blumenvase, der Kühlschrank, der Stuhl, das Feuer, das Radio.

praktisch, weich, bunt, elektrisch, lang, hoch, schön, gross, tief, zuverlässig, bequem, neu.

Exercise 4 (b)

Put into English:

1. Hat Ihr Nachbar ein neues Auto? 2. Ach, wir haben kein frisches Brot. 3. Ist jener kleine Laden offen? Ich

möchte eine saftige Apfelsine. 4. Karls neuer Wecker rasselt; er schläft lange heute morgen. 5. Dieses hübsche Mädchen zeigt mir ihre kleine Puppe. 6. Was hast du in der Tasche, Hans? Ich habe mein scharfes Taschenmesser, einen rostigen Schlüssel, dieses schmutzige Taschentuch und eine kaputte Uhr. 7. Bringen Sie mir ein reines Trinkglas! 8. Karl zerbricht jenen grossen Krug. 9. Ein kleiner Dackel holt meinen neuen

Ball. 10. Meine alte Grossmutter liest nicht; sie strickt einen grünen Pullover.

Exercise 4 (c)

Complete:

1. Mei— klein— Bruder schwimm— nicht. 2. Hämmer— S— n—— so laut! 3. W— arbeit— d— alt— Gärtner? 4. Dies— weiss— Hund l—f— n——. 5. D— Putzfrau tr— ei— leer— Eimer.

Put into German:

6. My old ruler is broken, but I have a new ball-point pen. 7. Don't go! Here is a very comfortable chair. 8. I would like to read, but my neighbour is showing us (uns) his new car. 9. Where is the new refrigerator? 10. Do you see that yellow bird?

Have a Try 4

Rendsheim ist ein kleines Dorf (village) in Deutschland. Nächste Woche verbringen wir dort unsere Ferien (holidays). Ein klarer Bach fliesst durch das schöne Dorf, und wir angeln und schwimmen im kühlen Wasser. Ich gehe auf ein breites Feld, wo ein alter Mann arbeitet. Ich pflücke einen roten Apfel in dem Obstgarten. Der Sommer ist wirklich die schönste Jahreszeit!

MAKING VERBS MORE INTERESTING.
HOW TO SAY "FOR", "INTO", ETC.

In this Lesson we are going to take two big steps forward. The first one concerns verbs.

We shall soon get tired of using only the Present Tense—"I go"; "do I see", etc. The most natural way and, in German, the easiest way to widen our scope is to learn "I want to go", "May I see ?", etc. Just think how often you use verbs of this kind every day.

As well as "want to" and "may", "*can*", "*must*", "*is (are) to*" and "*would like to*" (in Lesson Four) make the same kind of improvement.

Let us see how easy they are to learn.

If we leave out for the moment the person du, there are only two words for "want(s) to": WILL and WOLLEN. WILL is used with ich, er, sie and es (any single person) and WOLLEN with wir, Sie and sie. There are no -e and -t endings with ich, er, sie and es, just the -EN with "we, you and they", and a change of vowel to watch. The other words of this type are just as simple. Here is the complete list:

	ich, er, sie, es	wir, Sie, sie
want to	will	wollen
may	darf	dürfen
can	kann	können
must (have to)	muss	müssen
am, is, are to	soll	sollen
would like to	möchte	möchten

Let us also learn the words for "SHALL" or "WILL":

ich WERDE   er, sie, es WIRD
wir, Sie, sie WERDEN

You can regard this as an addition to the above list, but with a separate form for ich, ending in the usual -e.

Now notice how these words work in a sentence:

May I borrow your penknife?, Darf ich Ihr Taschenmesser
borgen?
That girl can sing nicely, Jenes Mädchen kann schön *singen*.
We are to go to bed early, Wir sollen früh zu Bett *gehen*.

With any person, the main verb (borrow, sing, buy, go) always
ends in -EN (it is in fact the *infinitive*), and instead of following
immediately after "may", "can", "want to", etc., it comes at
the *end* of the sentence.

You do not say Ich kann spiel*e*, er muss geh*t*.

Have you realised the special importance of werde, wird and
werden? When we say Ich werde spielen, er wird geben, we
have without any extra effort made a new tense, the FUTURE
tense of spielen and geben. To make the future tense of any
verb in the language all you have to do is to put its infinitive
after one of these three words.

How to say "for", "into", etc.

The second thing you will like to know at this stage is how
to make up expressions such as "for my sister" and "into the
shop".
"For" and "into" are called *prepositions*, and you have
already met some of these very useful words in the Have a Try
pieces. For a start we will learn only eight:

durch, through	für, for (on behalf of)
gegen, against	um, around
ohne, without	auf, on to (flat surfaces)
in, into	an, (up) to (nearby points)

There is a good reason for this limit; prepositions cause
most of the other "endings" we have to learn, but these eight
are easy. They affect only der words, changing the der, ein,

dieser, etc. to den, einen, diesen—in fact we need the "*object endings*" again, which we have already learnt.

So we shall say:

> in das Haus; gegen die Mauer; but in *den* Garten: für meine Schwester; durch das Feuer; but ohne *einen* Schlüssel.

We shall refer to the above prepositions as List 1.

How to say "I like swimming"

"I like swimming" (or "I like to swim") is put as follows:

> Ich schwimme *gern* (literally "I swim gladly")

Similarly, "he likes reading" is er liest gern and "I like to go to the pictures" is Ich gehe gern in das (ins) Kino.

Word List 5

der Wald, the wood	dicht, thick (of woods, etc.)
der Wind, the wind	draussen, outside
der Zug, the train	verlassen, to leave (places)
das Kino, the cinema	giessen, to pour

Exercise 5 (*a*)

Change the verbs in the following sentences to the form asked for in the brackets:

1. Dieses Mädchen tanzt gut. (can dance well) 2. Ich suche ein gutes Hotel. (must look for) 3. Kaufen Sie einen roten Farbstift? (do you want to buy) 4. Der Zug verlässt den Bahnhof. (will leave) 5. Wir hören das Radio. (would like to hear)

Put into English:

6. Wir sollen nicht rauchen. 7. Ein Hund kann nicht fliegen. 8. Wird Ihre Schwester die grüne Blumenvase bringen? 9. Dürfen wir heute morgen ins (in das) Dorf gehen? 10. Mein Grossvater liest gern die Zeitung.

Exercise 5 (b)

Put into German:

1. Would you like to meet my brother? 2. A joiner can make a table. 3. You may pour some (etwas) water into my tumbler. 4. I shall look for my hotel. 5. We must go through this thick wood. 6. My little dog wants to play outside; he goes to the door. 7. Can you fetch the bread? 8. Every girl would like to have a nice doll. 9. I can't write without a pen. 10. Our

neighbour likes fishing. 11. The bread falls on to the carpet.
12. That bird flies against the wind.

Exercise 5 (c)

Put the prepositions in this Lesson in front of as many
suitable nouns as you can find in the Word Lists

e.g. ohne einen Ball, für meine Schwester, in den Kleiderschrank

Have a Try 5

Mein deutscher Brieffreund will uns nächstes Jahr in
London besuchen. Er lernt seit drei Jahren Englisch und
schickt mir oft einen sehr interessanten Brief aus Hamburg.
Er ist von Schiffen und Dampfern begeistert (keen). Auch

rudert er gern. Wir werden sicher viel Zeit an der Themse verbringen (spend).

LESSON SIX

"WITH", "TO" AND "FROM"

Here are eight more prepositions which we shall refer to as List 2:

mit, with	aus, out of
nach, to (destinations) and after	in, in
	auf, on (flat surfaces)
von, from	an, at points or on *walls*, etc.
zu, to (usually people)	

These prepositions are kept together because they have a special effect on the words which follow them. Look at the examples below and see what happens to "the", "a" and all the words which replace them:

> mit einem Ball; nach dieser Stadt; auf meinem Tisch; aus jenem Hotel; an der Tür; von einem Garten

There are only two endings to learn, -EM on *any* word used with a der or das noun and -ER if the noun is a die word.

If an adjective is added, it will in every case end in -EN, according to our rule about adjectives following a "changed" first word (Lesson Three).

> e.g. in ein*em* dicht*en* Wald

Whilst we are talking about the prepositions in List 2 there are three interesting things to note:

(i) in dem, an dem, zu dem and von dem are often shortened to im, am, zum and vom. Der is treated like this in only one place: after zu. Zu der can be written zur;

(ii) instead of having to learn different words for "in" and "into", "on" and "on to", "at" and "up to", you will notice that IN, AUF and AN are used in both cases, but with different endings;

(iii) sometimes it is not the ending, but the choice of the right preposition which is difficult, so it would be a good idea to learn by heart a few phrases made with unexpected prepositions:

in the country, *auf* dem Land
in the sky, *am* Himmel
at home, *zu* Haus(e)
(to) home, *nach* Haus(e)
at school, the theatre and other buildings, *in* der Schule, *im* Theater
in the morning, evening, etc., *am* Morgen, Abend, etc.
on the wireless, *im* Radio
to buildings, *in die* Schule, *in das* Kino, etc.

Nicht wahr?

In English we have a habit of ending questions with "isn't it?", "don't you?", "can't we?" and similar expressions. There is a useful oddment in German which stands for *all* these: it is nicht wahr?, which really means ist das nicht wahr? ("is that not true?")

Thus you can say Sie kommen morgen, nicht wahr?, Das ist Ihr Bruder, nicht wahr? and so on.

Word List 6

der Arzt, the doctor	hängen, to hang
der Vorhang, the curtain	schneiden, to cut
die Garage, the garage	morgen, tomorrow
die Milch, the milk	scharf, sharp
die Sonne, the sun	Herr Mr.
das Frühstück, the breakfast	Frau Schmidt, Mrs. Smith
das Land, the country	Fräulein Miss
das Pult, the desk	
das Schlafzimmer, the bedroom	

Exercise 6 (a)

Complete:

1. Ist H—— Schneider — Hause? 2. F—— Schmidt m—— in d— Küche arbeit—. 3. Karl komm— mit sei—— klein— Bruder aus jen— grün— Wald. 4. Ei— Blumenvase steh— in dies— Zimmer —— d— Tisch, n——

w——? 5. Fräu—— Kleber sitz— — Fenster. 6. Ich wander— nicht g—— durch d— tief— Schnee.

Exercise 6 (*b*)

Put into German:

1. I must write a letter with my new ball-point pen. 2. Mrs. Meyer is cutting the bread with a sharp knife. 3. Can you see a key on my desk? 4. My little dog runs out of the room. 5. Mr. Kleber is sleeping in a comfortable bed. 6. I must go to the doctor tomorrow. 7. You would like to live in the country, wouldn't you? 8. I am to work in the garden after (the) breakfast. 9. Mr. Meyer from the hotel wants to speak to your brother. 10. My alarm clock stands on a little table in my bedroom.

Exercise 6 (*c*)

"Where do they all belong?"

Arrange the words below to form ten correct sentences:

Der Gärtner			— Teller
Mein Lineal			— Wand
Ein Vorhang		auf	— Himmel
Die Milch	liegt	in	— Garten
Ein Bild	steht	aus	— Kühlschrank
Das Trinkglas	hängt	an	— Löschblatt
Das Brot	kommt	mit	— Fenster
Unser Auto			— Tisch
Ein Zug			— Bahnhof
Die Sonne			— Garage

Have a Try 6

Underline the "odd word out" in each line:

1. Tisch, Stuhl, Bett, Baum, Büfett.
2. Apfel, Apfelsine, Birne, Banane, Blatt.
3. Zug, Auto, Brücke, Flugzeug, Wagen.
4. Bleistift, Tinte, Kugelschreiber, Feder, Farbstift.
5. Postamt, Kino, Rathaus, Marktplatz, Theater.
6. Freund, Vater, Tante, Mutter, Onkel.
7. Hund, Katze, Maus, Pferd, Fliege.
8. Schuh, Hut, Tischtuch, Jacke, Hemd.

A NEW SENTENCE-PATTERN. HOW TO SAY
"I GET UP" and "I GO TO SLEEP"

Now for a useful new kind of sentence. It is connected with the phrases we have just been learning—auf dem Tisch, am Morgen, etc.

In both German and English a sentence becomes more interesting if we start off with one of these phrases: just think of the old favourite "Once upon a time . . .".

In German something special happens when we do this. Look at these examples:

> "In the café I eat my lunch", Im Café *esse ich* zu Mittag
> "At school we have to learn maths", In der Schule *müssen wir* Mathematik lernen

No, these are not questions. If a phrase starts the sentence, the *verb* must be the next word, and if there are *two* verbs, this means the *muss* or *kann* type of verb we had in Lesson Five.

Learn this simple rule and you will have grasped one of the most important things in making up German sentences.

Have you noticed that phrases always tell *when* (in der Nacht), *where* (auf dem Tisch) or *how* (mit einem Lineal) something is done?

Instead of auf dem Tisch we could say dort ("there") and for in der Nacht we could put dann ("then"). There are in fact quite a number of *single words* telling "when", "where" and "how" that we ought to learn next.

Remember, like the phrases they must have the *verb next* if they begin a sentence.

Here they are:

"when"	*"where"*	*"how"*
jetzt, now	hier, here	plötzlich, suddenly
dann, then	dort or da, there	schnell, quickly
einmal, once	unten, downstairs,	langsam, slowly
endlich, finally	below	natürlich, naturally,
		of course

"when"	*"where"*	*"how"*
bald, soon	oben, upstairs, above	leise, quietly
spät, late	draussen, outside	traurig, sadly
schon, already	überall, everywhere	
oft, often	nirgends, nowhere	

Some words that we already know (heute, nebenan, etc.) can be added to this list.

How to say "I get up" and "I go to sleep"

We already know that stehen is "to stand". "To get up" is *auf*stehen. A lot of useful new verbs can be made like this, by adding an extra word to a verb you already know. Here are some:

*ein*schlafen, to go to sleep	*auf*gehen, to rise (of sun, etc.)
*an*kommen, to arrive	*vor*lesen, to read aloud

When you use them, the verb is in its usual place, but the extra word is taken off and put at the *end* of the sentence. Thus:

> Die Grossmutter *schläft* auf ihrem Stuhl *ein*
> Bald *kommt* der Zug aus Hamburg *an*

Notice that when a verb such as kann, muss or wird is used, the infinitive and its extra word stay together:

> Ich *werde* in meinem bequemen Bett *einschlafen*

Word List 7

der Organist, the organist
die Aufgabe, the exercise
die Orgel, the organ
die Mathematik, mathematics
die Schere, the scissors
die Wolle, the wool
das Büro, the office (in das Büro = "to work")
das Café, the café
das Dach, the roof
das Fernsehprogramm, the television programme
das Mittagessen, the lunch
das Modellflugzeug, the model aeroplane
das Speiseeis, the ice-cream
ansehen, to look at
jemand, someone

Exercise 7 (*a*)

Auf dem Gasherd; Mit seinem Modellflugzeug; Nach dem Frühstück; Mit der Schere; In der Kirche

Rewrite the following sentences, beginning each one with the most suitable phrase from this list. Remember where the *verb* will come!

1. Mein kleiner Bruder spielt im Garten. 2. Meine Mutter schneidet die Wolle. 3. Der Organist spielt die Orgel. 4. Ich muss in das Büro gehen. 5. Wir kochen das Mittagessen.

Draussen; Jetzt; Am Morgen; Am Abend; Langsam

Put the correct phrase or word from this list at the beginning of the following sentences and rewrite them. Remember, *verb* next!

6. Ich springe gern aus dem Bett. 7. Wir sitzen zu Hause und sehen uns das Fernsehprogramm an. 8. Ich schreibe diese Aufgabe. 9. Ein Zug muss in den Bahnhof einfahren. 10. Ich kann im Wald wandern.

Exercise 7 (*b*)

Put into German:

1. On the roof I can see a bird. 2. Read me (mir) your letter aloud. 3. Of course I go to sleep after my supper. 4. Downstairs someone is making the breakfast. 5. Now I must get up.

Rewrite with the *italicized* words first:

1. Schnee liegt *überall*. 2. Das Mädchen spricht *leise* mit ihrer Grossmutter. 3. Ich muss *oft* Brot im Laden holen. 4. Mein Hund darf *in der Küche* schlafen. 5. Die Sonne wird *bald* aufgehen.

Have a Try 7

In Berlin fährt man gern mit der Untergrundbahn. Oft muss man stehen und an einer Strippe hängen. Aber mit dem Autobus geht es nicht so schnell. An jeder Haltestelle steigen Leute ein und aus.

In einem U-Bahnwagen kann man ein Buch lesen, wenn die Reise ziemlich lange dauert. Natürlich darf man in einem vollen Wagen keine Zeitung ausbreiten!

LESSON EIGHT

ABOUT PLURALS

It is really time we found out how to make nouns plural. First let us see why we have not done so before.

If nouns added -S as in English, there would be no difficulty. But only a few German words of foreign origin do this— "Cafés", "Hotels", "Autos", for example. Most German nouns behave rather like the odd English words "children", "mice", "men" and "sheep".

What actually happens can be seen from the following examples: if you learn them, these seven words will give you a handy summary of all the possibilities:

chairs = *Stühle*	letters = *Briefe*	glasses = *Gläser*
doors = *Türen*	windows = *Fenster*	children = *Kinder*
	streets = *Strassen*	

You will see that instead of -S you have to choose one of the following endings:

$$\text{-E} \qquad \text{-ER} \qquad \text{-(E)N}$$

In addition, one-syllable words containing "a", "o" or "u" usually add ·· along with -E or -ER (but never with -N), and Fenster shows that some words, like the English "sheep", don't change at all.

All we need to know now is which of these ways of making the plural to choose for any given word. This depends mainly on whether the noun is a der, die or das word—thus -N is added to most die words, whilst ·· -ER is typical of das words.

The best thing is to put all this in a kind of table:

	der words	*die words*		*das words*
Add:	-E	-(E)N	(i)	-ER
	(+ ·· on a, o, u			(+ ·· on a, o, u)
	in one-syllable words		(ii)	-E
	only)			(words with no
				a, o, u)

Exceptions:

Männer	⎱ (like das	Hände	⎱	
Wälder	⎰ words)	Wände	⎰ (like der	
Hunde		Städte	⎰ words)	
Schuhe	(no ··)	Mütter		
Tage		Töchter		
Arme				

Exceptions:

Hände	⎱	
Wände	⎰ (like der	
Städte	⎰ words)	
Mütter		
Töchter		

Exceptions:

Kinder	⎫	
Bilder	⎬ (-er,	
Lichter	⎬ though	
Lieder	⎬ no ··)	
Eier		
Felder	⎭	
Jahre	(not ·· -er)	
Betten	⎱ (like die	
Hemden	⎰ words)	

Der and das words ending in -EL, -EN, -ER, -CHEN or -LEIN add *nothing*, except in some cases an ·· over a, o or u.

Almost *every* word ending in -E adds -N (including der Junge, das Auge, etc.).

. . . . .

Refer to this scheme as you try your luck in the exercises below. To master German plurals you will need patience, but a good start is half the battle. Here are three more useful hints:

(i) Das words *never* add ·· and -E.

(ii) Words such as der Brief and der Tisch add -E, NOT -EN (as you will be tempted to imagine)

(iii) *NO* words add ·· along with -N.

. . . . .

Now for one or two final facts about plurals before you begin to use them in sentences.

(*a*) "The" with plurals of all genders is DIE (just as "les" replaces "le" and "la" in French).

This die remains unchanged if the noun is the object or follows a preposition in List 1. But after a preposition in List 2 it becomes DEN and the noun adds an extra -N, unless it already ends with -n. Here is a sentence to explain this:

Die Kinder hören *die* Vögel in *den* Bäumen

(*b*) Very often a plural noun needs *no* introductory word. "Friends" are just Freunde; "girls play with dolls" would be Mädchen spielen mit Puppen. The words ein, eine and einen disappear in the plural, as you can see from the English sentence "A dog is an animal". The plural is simply "Dogs are animals"; in German, Hunde sind Tiere.

(*c*) Two very useful words to put with plurals are einige (some) and viele (many, lots of). These end in -E because they replace DIE. For the same reason "these", "those", "my", "his", etc. with plurals will be dies*e*, jen*e*, mein*e*, sein*e*. Remember, after a preposition in List 2 all these words will need an extra -N because then they will be replacing den, not die.

(*d*) "New books", "old shoes" etc. are neu*e* Bücher, alt*e* Schuhe. But after plural die, diese, meine etc. adjectives need -EN

e.g. die neu*en* Bücher.

Nouns which are really two words (Tischtuch, Bahnhof) make only the second half plural (Tischtücher, Bahnhöfe). We do exactly the same thing with English words such as *rainbow, classroom*.

Word List 8

der Berg, the mountain	das Feld, the field
der Fluss, the river	das Licht, the light
der Kirchturm, the church tower	das Lied, the song
der Schuh, the shoe	das Hemd, the shirt
der Tag, the day	das Jahr, the year
die Brücke, the bridge	das Schloss, the castle
die Wolke, the cloud	wachsen, to grow
das Ei, the egg	

Exercise 8 (*a*)

Write the plural of:

dieser Schlüssel; meine Tasche; der Stuhl; das Land; eine
Aufgabe; jenes Bild; das Pferd; dieser Kirchturm; welcher Zug;
das Schloss.

Exercise 8 (*b*)

der braune Hund   ein brauner Hund   braune Hunde

Use the following nouns in the same way and put with each
one an adjective of your own choice:

der Berg, das Licht, der Fluss, die Brücke, die Wolke, der Teller,
das Haus, der Tennisball, das Trinkglas, die Banane.

Exercise 8 (*c*)

Put into English:

1. An den Wänden hängen schöne Bilder. 2. Die weissen
Wolken ziehen über die grünen Felder. 3. Meine Brüder
haben Bleistifte, Messer und Taschentücher in den Taschen.

Complete:

4. Hinter dies— klein— Dörf—— seh— wir gross— Berg—. 5. In d— blau— Vase— sehe ich bunt— Blume—. 6. Gross— Bäum— wachsen in jen— schön— Wäld——.

Put into the plural:

7. Eine Apfelsine liegt auf meinem Teller. 8. Ein schönes Auto steht in unserer Garage. 9. Ich kann einen reifen Apfel an jenem Baum sehen. 10. Jenes Kind singt ein schönes Lied.

Have a Try 8

Der Rhein ist ein berühmter deutscher Fluss. Viele Menschen machen Ausflüge mit den Rheindampfern. An den Ufern sehen sie Schlösser. Mit einer Kamera kann man allerlei Aufnahmen machen. Später zeigt man sie seinen Freunden. Dörfer, Städte und Weinberge liegen nicht weit vom Fluss. Auch kann man lange Wanderungen durch kühle Wälder machen.

MORE PREPOSITIONS. HOW TO SAY "ME", "HIM", ETC.

Prepositions are such useful words that we will deal now with our last group:

über (over, above)	vor (before, in front of)
unter (under)	hinter (behind)
zwischen (between)	neben (near, beside)

We will call this List 3.
The following sentences show how they are used:

Ich *laufe* hinter ein*en* Baum : ich *stehe* hinter ein*em* Baum
Ich *wohne* neben *der* Kirche : ich *gehe* neben *die* Kirche
Das Auto *wartet* vor *dem* Haus : das Auto *fährt* vor *das* Haus vor

You will see that when these prepositions indicate the *position* in which a thing or person *is*, *lies* or *stands* they behave like those in List 2. But when they indicate *movement* (*going* behind, *moving* or *putting* near to something) they cause "*object endings*" like the prepositions in List 1.

Notice that when über suggests movement it really means "across":

ich gehe über die Strasse, über eine Brücke

With object endings, it can also mean "about" (a subject)

e.g. ich spreche über die Ferien (= holidays)

How to say "me", "him", etc.

We already know the words for "I", "he", "she" and so on. But we cannot say "He sees I" or "for he" (i.e. when the pronoun is an object or comes after a preposition). We need the words for "me", "him", "her", etc.

The trouble is that German has *two* words to choose between in cases such as this. The following table will show you what to do:

	As object or after preposition of List 1 type	After prepositions of List 2 type
me	mich	mir
him	ihn	ihm
her	sie	ihr
you	Sie	Ihnen
them	sie	ihnen

"us" is always UNS

ihn and sie can mean "it" when referring to der and die *things* used as the *object* in a sentence. But after prepositions "it" is treated as follows:

"with it", "on it", "through it", etc. (*any* gender) become DAmit, DArauf, DAdurch, etc. (literally "therewith", "thereon", "therethrough").

The "r" separates two vowels (darin, daraus, etc.).

It is worth noting that these words with DA can also mean "with *them*", "in *them*", etc. so long as *things* are being spoken of. "With them" (people) must always be mit *ihnen*.

Now let us learn Word List 9 and do some exercises which include the above points and some more plurals.

Word List 9

der Badeanzug, the bathing costume
der Kopf, the head
der Zahn, the tooth
der Zaun, the fence
die Briefmarke, the stamp
die Mütze, the cap
das Geld, the money
das Haustier, the domestic animal
das Wörterbuch, the dictionary

kleben, to stick
kriechen, to creep
stecken, to put (into pockets, etc.)
nützlich, useful

Exercise 9 (*a*)

Put into German:

1. For us. 2. I would like to meet you. 3. Fetch them!
4. Can you hear me? 5. Without her. 6. With me. 7. Ask her!
8. I'm sitting beside you. 9. Out of it. 10. For me.

Exercise 9 (*b*)

Complete:

1. Ich muss ein— Briefmarke auf dies— Brief kleb—.
2. Der Vater h—lt seine Pfeife zwischen d— Zähn—.
3. Ich setze mein— Mütze auf d— Kopf. 4. Der Hund
l—ft über d— Teppich und kriecht unter ein— Stuhl.
5. Ein Taxi hält (= stops) vor d— Bahnhof.

Exercise 9 (*c*)

Put into the plural:

1. Hinter diesem hohen Zaun liegt ein schöner Garten.
2. Im Schaufenster sehe ich einen bunten Badeanzug. 3. Eine

weisse Wolke zieht über das grüne Feld. 4. An der Wand
hängt ein schönes Bild. 5. Mein kleiner Bruder will ein neues
Spielzeug kaufen.

Put into German:

1. Pour the milk into a glass. 2. Put this money in your
pocket. 3. Dictionaries are useful; we look for words in them.

4. Dogs are domestic animals. 5. Do you see that table?
There are blue flowers on it.

Have a Try 9

Bei heissem Wetter gehen wir alle in das Schwimmbad.
Jungen und Mädchen in bunten Badeanzügen schwimmen
oder plätschern im klaren Wasser. Die grösseren Jungen
tauchen mutig vom Sprungbrett, aber die kleineren Kinder
haben Angst davor, den Boden unter den Füssen zu verlieren.

Nach einer halben Stunde sind wir oft müde. Dann sitzen wir gern am Rand des Beckens und sehen den tüchtigeren Schwimmern zu.

HOW TO SAY "OF".   SOME REVISION

In English we use lots of expressions such as "the end of the road", "the top of the hill", in which OF appears to be just another preposition similar to "on" or "at".

But if we put these expressions into German, "OF" is not translated as a separate word. We must say

Das Ende der Strasse   and   Der Gipfel des Hügels

Similarly, "the door of the room" and "the roofs of the houses" would be

Die Tür des Zimmers   and   Die Dächer der Häuser

So, to say "OF THE", instead of putting a word in front of der, die and das, we *change* der and das to DES and die (singular and plural) to DER.

After DES (but not DER) the noun adds an S as well, rather like our 's in "my brother*s* bicycle". If the noun ends in S already, we add -ES

e.g. Die Tür des Hauses

All the words which replace "the" imitate DES and DER.

"of a" = ein*ES* (with der and das words) or ein*ER* (with die words)
"of that" (or those) = jenES or jenER (with die words and plurals)
"of my" = meinES or meinER (with die words and plurals)

and so on.

Remember, with eines, meines, etc. (all the words ending in S), the noun will add an S too, as after DES.

Adjectives following *any* of these changed words will add -EN (see our rule in Lesson Four)

e.g. Die Tür des grossen Zimmers
Der Name ihrer schönen Schwester

Study this carefully and you will have learnt the last of the "endings" which are so important—and troublesome in German.

Here are two more interesting things concerning "OF":

1. Willy's mother, *Willis* Mutter. Gisela's doll, *Giselas* Puppe.

Persons' names are treated exactly as in English except that the apostrophe is left out.

But "my uncle's car" or "this dog's collar" MUST be translated as "the car of my uncle", "the collar of this dog".

2. In expressions of *quantity* such as "a pound of apples", "a glass of water" or "a piece of bread" the "OF" is omitted. The German is

ein Pfund Äpfel; ein Glas Wasser; ein Stück Brot

At this stage you should spend some time thoroughly going over everything that happens with *objects*, *plurals* and after the various *prepositions*.

The exercises which follow practise not only "OF", but all the endings together.

Word List 10

der Briefkasten, the letter-box	ausziehen, to take off (shoes, clothes)
der Briefträger, the postman	
der Gipfel, the top (of mountains)	klettern, to climb
der Nähkasten, the work-basket	berühmt, famous
der Spaziergang, the walk	nass, wet
die Ecke, the corner	sofort, at once
die Schale, the peel	
die Rose, the rose	

Exercise 10 (a)

Use "of" to combine each of the following "pairs". The first one is done for you as an example.

    das Haus   mein bester Freund
         (das Haus mein*es* best*en* Freund*s*)
    die Schubkarre   der alte Gärtner

der Kugelschreiber	mein kleiner Bruder
die Tür	jener grosse Kleiderschrank
die Orgel	diese schöne Kirche
das Wasser	ein tiefer Fluss
die Schere	meine alte Grossmutter
die Zweige	die grünen Bäume
der Hut	jenes hübsche Mädchen
die Farbstifte	die kleinen Kinder
die Räder	unser neues Auto

Exercise 10 (b)

Complete:

1. In d— Schaufenster dies— modern— Laden— kann ich ei— elektrisch— Kühlschrank seh—.

2. D— Schwester jen— berühmt— Arzt— steckt rot— Rose— in ei— bunt— Blumenvase.

3. Nach ei—— lang— Spaziergang durch d— herbstlich— Wäld— muss ich mein— nass— Schuh— sofort auszuziehen.

4. Hungrig— Leute sitzen an d— bequem— Tisch— i— Speisezimmer dies— neu— Hotel—.

5. Über d— hoh— Mauer d— lang— Garten— klettert ei— schmutzig— Junge und sucht sei—— Ball unter d— Blume—.

Exercise 10 (*c*)

Put into German:

1. The postman opens the letter-box with a big key. 2. Our little dog likes to lie on my brother's bed. 3. I often buy an ice-cream in the little café at the corner of our street. 4. Would

you like a glass of milk? 5. Do you find your sister's dictionary useful? 6. I never eat the peel of an apple. 7. The white clouds float (ziehen) over the tops of the high mountains. 8. Fetch the sharp scissors out of my work-basket. 9. In front of the big windows of my bedroom white curtains are hanging. 10. A fine tree with green leaves is growing in the doctor's garden.

Have a Try 10

Eine Gruppe Kinder macht eine Wanderung auf dem Land. Der Weg führt durch Wälder und Dörfer, aber endlich sehen sie neben einem schönen Fluss die hell erleuchteten Fenster eines modernen Gebäudes.

Das ist die Jugendherberge. Man schreibt seinen Namen in ein grosses Buch und zeigt seine Mitgliedskarte. Dann darf man sich an den langen Tisch setzen und ein gutes Abendessen erwarten. In einem anderen Zimmer kann man Schach oder Karten spielen.

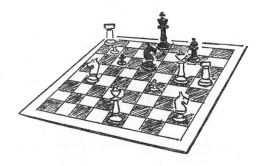

LESSON ELEVEN

SOME NUMBERS. GIVING, TELLING AND SHOWING

Here is something easy after all the hard work of the first ten Lessons! Let's learn some numbers, just from 1 to 30 for a start. We all need to know numbers, especially in connection with money and dates and for telling the time, which will come later.

1. The only numbers that you really have to learn by heart are 1 to 12:

ein(s), 1	fünf, 5	neun, 9
zwei, 2	sechs, 6	zehn, 10
drei, 3	sieben, 7	elf, 11
vier, 4	acht, 8	zwölf, 12

Note: ein will sometimes appear as ein*s* (when no other word follows it).

Watch the spelling of zw*ei*, d*rei*, v*ier* and s*ie*ben.

2. For -TEEN all we do is to add -ZEHN to the numbers already learnt:

dreizehn, 13	se*ch*zehn, 16 (Note: no s)
vierzehn, 14	sie*b*zehn, 17 (Note: no en)
fünfzehn, 15	achtzehn, 18
	neunzehn, 19

3. For -TY add -ZIG to the original numbers.

(vierzig will be 40, fünfzig 50, and so on)

*ZWAN*zig, 20, is slightly irregular, but this brings it even closer to the English.

4. How do we get from 21 to 30? We know the numbers already. It is just a matter of putting them together, and this is how it is done:

21, einundzwanzig 22, zweiundzwanzig 23, dreiundzwanzig and so on up to neunundzwanzig, 29

50

Just think of "four and twenty blackbirds" and do all the intermediate German numbers in that order.

5. "30" tries to cheat! It is drei*SS*ig, not dreizig. It is the only -TY *not* to have -ZIG.

To make the practising of numbers more interesting we can learn the words for "plus", "minus", etc. Here they are:

plus, und	minus, weniger
times, mal	divided by, durch

e.g. $6 \times 4 = 24$ is sechsmal vier *ist* (or *macht*) vierundzwanzig

We can also revise the plurals of nouns by putting them with numbers. But notice that units of currency, weight, length, etc., are as a rule *not* made plural.

So "15 Marks" is fünfzehn *Mark* and "2 lb." is zwei *Pfund*.

Giving, telling and showing

Verbs of this kind, which we need every day, will go wrong in German unless you know the secret of their use.

In English we can say:

"I give a bone to the dog" *or* "I give the dog a bone"
"I show some stamps to my friend" *or* "I show my friend some stamps"

In German we must *always* use the second construction, thus:

Ich gebe *dem Hund einen Knochen*
Ich zeige *meinem Freund einige Briefmarken*

The secret is to leave out "*to*" and put the *person* before the *thing*.

But notice that the endings *dem* Hund and mein*em* Freund show the zu to be understood, although it is not actually there. This is of course equally true of the English version: if you think a moment, you will see that we are not "giving the dog" to anyone.

This German construction is used with all similar verbs, such as "explaining", "offering" and "presenting", when "to a person" does not indicate any *movement towards* him. When a verb which does involve movement is used, zu is kept in.

"I *go to* the doctor" would be Ich *gehe zum* Arzt

Word List 11

der Fuss, the foot	das Kilometer, the kilometre
der Grad, the degree	das Nest, the nest
der Matrose, the sailor	das Rad, the wheel
die Geschichte, the story	anbieten, to offer
die Wahrheit, the truth	erzählen, to tell, relate
	schenken, to give (as a present)
	reichen, to hand, pass

Exercise 11 (*a*)

Give the German (in words) for:

17, 27, $7 \times 3 = 21$, $15 - 4 = 11$, $3 + 9 = 12$, $30 \div 2 = 15$, $19 - 5 = 14$, $6 + 10 = 16$, $24 \div 3 = 8$, $6 \times 5 = 30$.

Exercise 11 (*b*)

Give the German for:

four wheels, twenty pounds, ten marks, three years, six feet, eight kilometres, five dogs, two pictures, three men, thirty degrees.

Exercise 11 (c)

Put into English:

1. Die Grossmutter schenkt dem kleinen Mädchen eine neue Uhr. 2. Hans sagt seiner Mutter die Wahrheit. 3. Geben Sie mir bitte meine Füllfeder! 4. Oft bringt der Dackel meinem Grossvater die Zeitung. 5. Der Arzt bietet meiner Tante einen Stuhl an.

Put into German:

6. The sailor tells a long story to the children. 7. The waiter brings my friend a glass. 8. Our neighbour offers my mother some flowers. 9. The boy shows the bird's nest to his sister. 10. Sometimes I have to hand my mother her glasses.

Have a Try 11

Es ist ein schöner Sommertag. Aus einem wolkenlosen Himmel strahlt die Sonne herunter. Schon drängt sich eine grosse Menge am Flussufer, denn (for, because) viele Mannschaften (crews) rudern heute auf dem Fluss. Zwei Boote liegen am Landungssteg, ein drittes (third) ist schon in Bewegung. Aus dem Bootshaus kommen junge Männer in kurzen Hosen, jeder mit einem weissen Pullover. Jetzt ergreifen sie die Ruder. Bald beginnt der Kampf!

LESSON TWELVE

HOW TO JOIN UP SENTENCES.
MORE NUMBERS

In this Lesson we are going to make an important addition to our stock of sentence-types—that is, a sentence made by linking together two shorter ones.

Suppose we look at the following statements:

> I have my breakfast.   I go to work.

So far, to join them we have only the choice of "and" or "then", which do not do the job very well. *"Before"* would be much more effective.

"Linking words" such as "before" are called *conjunctions* (think of a road *junction*), and here is a list of the most useful ones:

before, ehe *or* bevor	whilst, während
as soon as, sobald	although, obgleich
when or if, wenn	until, bis
because, weil	whether, ob
	that, dass

You need not learn all these at once: the list is here to refer to as you do the later exercises.

Now let us see how these conjunctions work:

> Ich esse mein Frühstück, *ehe ich* in das Büro *gehe*.
> Ich esse, *wenn ich* hungrig *bin*.

They send the verb to the *end* of the part of the sentence that they introduce, and this part must be marked off by a *comma*.

Look at this further example:

> Ich suche meine Füllfeder, *weil ich* einen Brief schreiben *will*.

You will see that when there are *two* verbs in the part introduced by the conjunction, the "can", "will", "must" type of verb is placed last.

54

Notice, none of the words is actually changed in this important new kind of sentence—just remember the *position* of the verb in the second half.

It is also a help to realise that the *subject* immediately follows the conjunction.

. . . . .

Here are the rest of the numbers we might need:

vierzig, 40   sie*b*zig, 70 (no en)

fünfzig, 50   achtzig, 80

se*ch*zig, 60 (no s)   neunzig, 90

a hundred, hundert (no ein needed)

200, 300, etc., zweihundert, dreihundert, etc.

1000, tausend   2000, zweitausend (and so on)

a million, eine Million (*N.B.* a noun)

and finally one really long number:

3457, dreitausendvierhundert*sie*benundfünfzig (*N.B.* no und after the hundert)

Word List 12

der Bahnsteig, the platform	kosten, to cost
der Fernsehapparat, the television set	entzückend, delightful
der Friseur, the hairdresser	leise, quiet(ly)
der Gottesdienst, the (church) service	noch, still
der Schläger, the bat (also racket, club, etc.)	schläfrig, sleepy
die Bewegung, movement, motion	so, so
die Butter, the butter	zu, too
die Schulaufgaben, homework	
das Abteil, the compartment	
das Haar, the hair (usually pl.: die Haare)	
(das) Kricket, cricket	
einsteigen in (+obj. ending), to get into (trains, etc.)	

Exercise 12 (a)

Find the correct sentence in Column 2 to match each of those in Column 1 and join them up, using a different conjunction in each case:

Column 1	Column 2
Ich gehe zum Friseur.	Mein Wecker rasselt am Morgen.
Ich stehe schnell auf.	Mein Vater liest die Zeitung.
Wir müssen auf dem Bahnsteig warten.	Ich bin nicht schläfrig.
Meine Grossmutter strickt einen Pullover.	Meine Haare sind zu lang.
Ich muss um zehn Uhr zu Bett gehen.	Der Zug kommt in den Bahnhof.

Exercise 12 (b)

Put into English:

1. Ich muss zum Sportgeschäft gehen, wenn ich einen neuen Tennisschläger kaufen will. 2. Wir dürfen nicht in ein Abteil

einsteigen, während der Zug noch in Bewegung ist. 3. Ich spiele oft Klavier, weil ich Musik so entzückend finde. 4. Der Organist spielt leise, bis der Gottesdienst beginnt. 5. Die Butter ist noch frisch, obgleich wir keinen Kühlschrank haben.

Put into German:

6. My grandfather is seventy-five years old. 7. This television-set costs DM 846 (846 marks). 8. I go straight to bed when I come home from the theatre. 9. This dog is so fat that it can't run. 10. Hans must do (machen) his homework before he plays cricket.

Have a Try 12

Finish these sentences with some words of your own choice. The first one is done for you.

1. Ich kann den Sportfunk hören, wenn ich ein schönes Radio habe.

2. Ich kann lesen, wenn . . .

3. Wir wollen in den Wald gehen, obgleich . . .

4. Zwei Hunde haben acht Beine, weil . . .

5. Wir sitzen immer im Garten, bis . . .

SOME CONVERSATION. HOW TO SAY "I PUT" AND "I ASK"

As we already know all the grammar that is involved, we could usefully learn by heart at this stage a few everyday remarks that you might make to people, or that people might make to you.

Guten Morgen! Guten Abend! Guten Tag! (*N.B.* "object" ending)
(Good morning. Good evening. Good day.)

Gute Nacht! (Good night, on going to bed)

Wie geht es Ihnen? (How are you?)
Sehr gut, danke, und Ihnen? (Very well, thank you, and you?)

                    wo
Können Sie mir bitte sagen, wie . . . (verb)?
                    was
                 where
(Can you please tell me how . . . ?)
                 what
  (*N.B.* wo, wie, was act here like conjunctions)

Wie komme ich nach (zu) . . . ?
(How do I get to . . . ?)

Gehen Sie geradeaus (links, rechts)!
(Go straight on, to the left, to the right)

Wieviel kostet . . . ?
(How much is . . . ?)

Was macht das?
(How much does that come to?)

Wie heisst . . . ?
(What is . . . called?)

Was haben Sie heute vor?
(What are you doing today?)

Was darf es sein?
(What can I do for you?)—in shops, etc.

Danke schön! Danke sehr! Vielen Dank!
(Thank you very much)

There is a useful word *man* which we ought to learn here. man sagt means "one says", "people say", "they say", when you have no particular person in mind. Hier spricht man Deutsch is translated as "German spoken here".

You will see that man is an addition to er, sie and es and has the same form of verb.

"I put" and "I ask"

These very common verbs are difficult in German for the beginner because you have to choose carefully which word you really need.

"I put the book on the desk" is Ich *lege* das Buch auf das Pult

For putting things on tables, the floor, etc., where they lie more or less *flat*, you must use LEGEN.

"I put the bottle on the table" is Ich *stelle* die Flasche auf den Tisch

When you stand a thing upright, on its base, you must use STELLEN.

"I put the money in my pocket" is Ich *stecke* das Geld in die Tasche

For putting things into pockets, drawers or any kind of container, you must use STECKEN.

. . . . .

          where   wo
"I ask a policeman how ..." is Ich *frage* ein*en* Polizisten, wie . . . (vb)
           if   ob

FRAGEN is also used with a direct question:

> Ich frage ihn: „Wo ist der Bahnhof?"
> (Notice how the inverted commas are written)

But "I *ask* my friend *for* a light" is Ich *bitte* meinen Freund *um* Feuer.

The verb is BITTEN and instead of für, which you might have expected, we use UM, another List 1 preposition.

"Ask the doctor to examine you thoroughly" is *Bitten* Sie den Arzt, *Sie* gründlich *zu* untersuchen.

Here again we use BITTEN, with a new construction of which you will hear more later in the book.

Finally, "I ask the doctor a question" is Ich *stelle* d*em* Arzt eine Frage.

(Notice that zu is left out, as explained in Lesson Eleven.)

Word List 13

der Gepäckträger, the porter
der Polizist, the policeman
die Frau, wife, woman
das Gemüse, the vegetable(s)
das Rathaus, the town-hall

ich mache (die) Einkäufe, I do the shopping
abfahren, to set off, depart
allerlei, all kinds of

Exercise 13 (a)

Put into English:

1. Können Sie mir bitte sagen, wie ich zum Rathaus komme? 2. Gehen Sie geradeaus, dann links um die Ecke, und so kommen Sie direkt zum Rathaus. 3. Oft bittet mich meine Frau, Einkäufe in der Stadt zu machen. 4. Ich muss einen Gepäckträger fragen, auf welchem Bahnsteig der neun-Uhr-

Zug abfährt. 5. Die Putzfrau stellt ihren Eimer in die Ecke des Zimmers. 6. Auf dem Markt kann man allerlei Gemüse kaufen. 7. Meine Frau bittet einen dicken Mann, das Fenster des Abteils zu schliessen.

Put into German:

8. Put your coat on the bed. 9. What is the boy next door called? 10. I put my shoes under a chair when I go to bed. 11. How much is that cricket-bat in the window? 12. Can you please tell me where I can buy a newspaper? 13. Put some fresh flowers in that vase. 14. Ask my brother to show you his new bicycle.

Exercise 13 (b)

Complete with any suitable words:

1. Man spielt Fussball . . . 2. In einem Wald kann man . . . 3. Der Junge steckt die Hand . . . 4. Auf den Tisch stellt die Frau . . . 5. Ich muss meine Schwester ——, wo . . .

Have a Try 13
Im Schuhgeschäft

Guten Morgen, Frau Schulze! Was darf es sein?

Guten Morgen! Ich möchte ein Paar braune Halbschuhe.

Ach ja, ich weiss noch, welche Grösse Sie haben. Versuchen Sie bitte dieses Paar—aus sehr gutem Leder, beste Qualität.

Leider sind sie mir zu eng. Haben Sie etwas Billigeres?

Wollen Sie bitte dieses Paar zu fünfundsechzig Mark anprobieren?

Diese hier sind ganz bequem. Ich nehme sie also.

Danke sehr. Sonst noch etwas?

Ja, eine Dose Schuhcreme, bitte.

Das macht sechsundsechzig Mark zwanzig, bitte. Danke schön.

Auf Wiedersehen!

ANOTHER WAY TO JOIN SENTENCES.
TELLING THE TIME IN GERMAN

In Lesson Twelve we learnt how to join up sentences by putting a conjunction in the *middle*. Have you noticed that we can join sentences equally well by putting the conjunction *first*?

> I wash myself *before* I get dressed

could also be written

> *Before* I get dressed, I wash myself

This gives us an extremely important type of sentence in German. Here is an example of it:

> *Wenn* ich hungrig *bin, esse* ich einen Apfel

The pattern is: CONJUNCTION . . . VERB, VERB . . .
Note the two verbs, one on each side of the comma. (We will limit ourselves for the time being to simple verbs, consisting of one word.) You can imagine this kind of sentence as a propeller with the comma as the hub.

. . . . .

You will remember meeting in Lesson 7 verbs such as *ein*schlafen and *an*kommen. Let us see how these are affected by conjunctions.

> Ich *stehe* früh am Morgen *auf*
> becomes   *Obgleich* ich früh am Morgen auf*stehe*

Really there is nothing new to learn. The *verb* (stehe) is placed last, according to our rule, and thus comes after the auf, which would normally be the final word. Notice that the two are then made into one word.

How to tell the time

Here is a practical use for some of our numbers. Times can be learnt very easily in three steps:

1. "o'clock" is Uhr.

Here we can use our original numbers 1 to 12. "It is ..." with times is always Es ist ..., so we can say at once Es ist ein Uhr, zwei Uhr, drei Uhr and so on up to zwölf Uhr.

2. "to" is vor: "past" is nach: "quarter" is Viertel: "minutes", Minuten. ("One minute" is eine Minute.)

Now we can use numbers up to 29. Read the following examples and make up some more for yourself:

fünf Minuten vor acht (Uhr, like the English "o'clock", is left out here): zwanzig Minuten nach zehn: Viertel vor elf: achtzehn Minuten nach eins: zehn Minuten vor vier.

3. "half past" is dealt with as follows:

3.30 is halb *vier*, 5.30 is halb *sechs*, 12.30 is halb *eins*, i.e. nach is not used and you count forward towards the *next* hour.

Learn also Mittag (mid-day) and Mitternacht (midnight). "AT" with times by the clock is UM, e.g. Um zwei Uhr.

Word List 14

der Name(n), the name	brauchen, to need
die Fahrkarte, the ticket	essen (*isst*), to eat
das Wartezimmer, the waiting-room	lösen, to buy (tickets)
	regnen, to rain
	so oft, every time, whenever

Exercise 14 (*a*)

Put into English:

1. Wenn meine Haare zu lang sind, gehe ich zum Friseur.
2. Obgleich es heute regnet, trage ich keine Mütze. 3. Um
halb fünf komme ich nach Hause. 4. Dieser Zug fährt um
Viertel vor zwei ab. 5. Ehe der Zug abfährt, löse ich meine
Fahrkarte.

Rewrite in German with the conjunction first:

6. Ich besuche meine Grossmutter, während ich im Dorf
bin. 7. Ich gehe früh zu Bett, weil ich früh aufstehe. 8. Ich
nehme ein Bad, so oft ich Fussball spiele. 9. Ich komme aus
der Kirche, wenn der Gottesdienst zu Ende ist. 10. Ich sitze
im Wartezimmer, bis der Arzt meinen Namen ruft.

Exercise 14 (*b*)

Write the following times in German (in words):

5.25; 11.40; 10.5; 6.15; 8 o'clock; 1.10; 2.30; 6.30; 3.45; 9 o'clock.

Exercise 14 (c)

Put into German:

1. When we need vegetables, we go to the market. 2. At half past seven the postman comes. 3. While the doctor eats his breakfast, he reads the newspaper. 4. Before the train reaches the station, it crosses a bridge. 5. Although Hans is 14 years old, he is very small.

Have a Try 14

Complete each sentence by underlining the correct word in brackets:

Ein Arzt arbeitet in einem (Wald, Museum, Krankenhaus).

Im Schuhgeschäft kaufe ich (Milch, Pantoffel, Tinte).

Zu Weihnachten bekomme ich (Geschenke, Zahnweh, einen Knochen).

Im Park spielen wir (die Orgel, Karten, Schlagball).

Ein Metzger verkauft (Hemden, Fleisch, Briefmarken).

Ein Pferd (singt, bellt, wiehert).

Eine Geige ist (ein Baum, ein Musikinstrument, ein Tier).

Ein Bettler bittet um (Gnade, ein Ei, Geld).

(Ein Koffer, ein Frosch, eine Kaffeekanne) steht auf dem Gasherd.

Ich trage einen Überzieher, wenn es (spät, kalt, billig) ist.

LESSON FIFTEEN

A NEW KIND OF SENTENCE. STILL MORE ABOUT CONJUNCTIONS. DAYS AND MONTHS

We have just been learning how to link two ideas in the same sentence by using a conjunction. Here is another useful way to do this without using one.

Instead of saying "I catch a bus, *because I want* to go to town" we can simply say "I catch a bus *to go* to town".

In German this is

Ich nehme einen Autobus, *UM* in die Stadt *ZU FAHREN*
(*not* . . . fahren in die Stadt)

It will help you to think of the UM as meaning "IN ORDER TO . . ." The other part ("GO") does not come immediately after it, but at the *end* of the sentence, and an extra ZU is put in before the verb.

In German, the pattern is always

UM . . . ZU ——EN

with the infinitive *last*. Make up some examples with different verbs at the end and memorize this construction.

Note: "I am going to speak, sneeze", etc. in the sense of "I am just *about to* . . ." is Ich WILL sprechen, etc.

This is simply another meaning of the word we learnt in Lesson Five.

. . . . .

Now for a final look at sentences beginning with a conjunction. *Learn* these examples:

Weil ich dieses Wort nicht verstehen *kann, suche* ich das Wörterbuch
(TWO verbs in the first half)

Obgleich Hans Fussball spielen *will, muss* er seine Aufgaben machen
(TWO verbs in each half)

66

There must always be a verb on each side of the comma. If the verb is one word, there is no difficulty. If you are using a "can", "must", "will" type of verb, this is the one to put in the indicated position.

. . . . .

Before we learn dates—the other main use for our numbers —here are the days of the week and the months in German:

Sonntag, Sunday	Donnerstag, Thursday
Montag, Monday	Freitag, Friday
Dienstag, Tuesday	Samstag *or*
Mittwoch, Wednesday	Sonnabend, Saturday

Notice the similarity to English. Do you see the connection between "thunder" (Donner) and the god Thor in "Thursday"?

Mittwoch ("mid-week") is made differently from the other words.

Januar	Juli
Februar	August
März	September
April	Oktober
Mai	November
Juni	Dezember

Except März, March, the months are either exactly like their English equivalents or have only *one* change of letter.

The Exercises in this Lesson contain some revision of material from previous chapters.

Word List 15

der Duft, the scent	ich mache eine Aufnahme, I take
der Fahrgast, the passenger	a photo
der Lehrer, the master, teacher	riechen, to smell
der Obstgarten, the orchard	sparen, to save (money)
die Mahlzeit, the meal	treiben, to drive
die Stelle, the place	wund, sore
das Wort, the word	
anknipsen, to switch on	

Exercise 15 (a)

Rewrite with the conjunction first:

1. Ich muss ein gutes Fahrrad haben, wenn ich schnell fahren will. 2. Ich muss mir die Hände waschen, ehe ich meine Mahlzeit essen darf. 3. Ich muss mein Geld sparen, weil ich einen neuen Tennisschläger kaufen will.

Put into German:

4. Although my brother can play the piano, he doesn't like singing. 5. While my wife is watching the television, she can knit. 6. Because the train is going to set off, the passengers are getting into the carriages. 7. We go into the orchard to pick apples. 8. You don't need an expensive camera to take good photos. 9. My sister fetches a knife to cut the bread. 10. I switch the wireless on to hear the news.

Exercise 15 (b)

Complete:

1. Auf d— Bahnsteig w—— ich ei—— Freund mei—— Brud—— treff—. 2. — sie—— Uhr rass—— mei— Wecker, — m—— aus d— Bett zu treib—. 3. I—

Juni k—— wir i— Garten d— Duft d— bunt—
Blumen riech—. 4. D— Kind— jene— klein— Schule
l—f— — vier Uhr aus d— Klassenzimmer—. 5. Zeig—
S— d— Arzt die wund— Stelle a— Kopf!

Put into the singular:

6. Fahrgäste lösen ihre Fahrkarten, ehe sie auf die Bahn-
steige gehen. 7. Im September finden die Gärtner reife Äpfel
unter den Bäumen.

Answer in German:

8. Was ist ein Pferd? 9. Wann fällt der Schnee? 10. Wo ist
die Schere?

Have a Try 15

Ein junger Komponist besucht den grossen Dirigenten
(conductor) Furtwängler in seinem Landhaus. „Ich möchte
Ihnen gern zwei Sätze (movements) aus meiner neuen Suite
‚Die Einsamen' vorspielen und Ihr Urteil darüber hören."

Während der Komponist spielt, sitzt Furtwängler neben
dem Klavier, um Bekanntschaft (acquaintance) mit den
„Einsamen" zu machen. Zwanzig Minuten später wendet
sich (turns) der Komponist zu Furtwängler und sagt: „Das
war (was) der eine Satz aus meiner Suite. Was halten Sie
davon, verehrter Meister?" „Ich ziehe die andere vor,"
antwortet Furtwängler trocken.

(vorziehen, to prefer)

HOW TO SAY "I TRY" AND "I FORGET".
DATES

Sentences ending with zu +infinitive—not only after um—
are a very common feature of German.

For instance,

Ich beginne *zu laufen* means "I start to run"

If we add something to explain where or how we run, the
zu laufen must still come last, so the extra words are placed in
front of it, after a comma.

Thus:

Ich beginne, sehr schnell *zu laufen*

"Try", "forget" and "ask" (see Lesson Thirteen) are three
more verbs that produce the same kind of sentence.

Die Katze *versucht*, einen Vogel *zu fangen*
(The cat *tries to catch* a bird)

Immer *vergesse* ich, meine Zeitung ins Büro *zu bringen*
(I always *forget to take* my newspaper to the office)

Ich muss meinen Onkel *bitten*, mit uns auf das Land *zu fahren*
(I must *ask* my uncle *to go* into the country with us)

Beginnen, versuchen, vergessen and bitten—these are the
four verbs followed by zu + infinitive which we will learn now.
Once you have mastered these, any others of the same kind
which occur later will seem quite easy.

Do you remember the word *ohne*, meaning "without"? This
too can be used with zu + infinitive.

ohne *zu sprechen* is the German for "without *speaking*"

So "without saying a word" would be *ohne* ein Wort *zu
sagen* and so on.

Dates

To be able to write the date in German, we must know, in addition to the days and months, the words for "four*th*", "ten*th*", "fifteen*th*", etc.

These are easily made from our original numbers. In English, you will notice, we add -TH. All we do in German is to add -T as far as "19th", and from "20th" onwards, -ST. (Zwanzigs*t* and dreissigs*t* would be too awkward to pronounce without the "s".)

Thus:

fünf*t* = 5th.   vierzehn*t* = 14th.   neunundzwanzigs*t* = 29th.

(Such words could, of course, be useful in many places, not only in dates. You might say, for example, "his twenty-first birthday".)

But how about "first", "second" and "third"? Well, these seem, worse luck, to break the rule both in English and in German. But they are less trouble in German. "Second" is zweit (literally "two-th"), so that at least is quite regular. The others must be learnt separately:

first = ERST   third = DRITT

Notice, too, that acht is used for "eighth" as well as "eight". As it ends in -t already, there is no need to add -t.

Now we are ready to use these numbers in dates. The most useful form of date is that which appears at the head of a letter or a newspaper, for example:

London, *den* zwei*ten* Mai | Montag, d*en* fünfundzwanzigs*ten* März

Note: (i) These dates are written with "object" endings. The number is treated as an adjective: following a "changed" first word, it must end in -en. (See Lesson Four.)

(ii) "Of" ("the second *of* May") is left out.

(iii) Whatever the English form ("May 2nd", "second of May", "2/5", etc.), the date in German must have this "formula":

ten
den ——sten (month)

You will also need to know "*ON* May 2nd", etc. This is

AM zweiten Mai, *AM* zehnten November, etc.

Finally there is the short form of the date in figures. It is written or printed like this:

Berlin, d. 2. Mai, am 9. April

Den is shortened to d. and another full-stop represents the -ten or -sten ending.

The day of the week and the year can, of course, be included in dates, as follows:

Freitag, den elften Januar neunzehnhunderteinundzwanzig

Word List 16

der Boxer, the boxer	bedecken, to cover
der Gegner, the opponent	fangen, to catch
der Ring, the ring	

Exercise 16 (*a*)

Write these dates in words, in German:

1. Tuesday, March 4th. 2. Sunday, June 27th. 3. London, 10th. December 1963. 4. 3:11:1951 5. On the fifth of November. 6. On May 1st. 7. Wednesday July 12th. 8. Saturday April 16th. 9. Bonn, 17th. Aug. 1872. 10. On February 2nd.

Exercise 16 (*b*)

Put into English:

1. Ich darf nicht vergessen, um vier Uhr zum Friseur zu gehen. 2. Im Café bittet eine Frau den Kellner, ihr ein Speiseeis zu bringen. 3. Dieser alte Briefträger versucht, die

Adresse ohne Brille zu lesen. 4. Im Oktober beginnen die Blätter, die Erde zu bedecken. 5. Ohne seinem Gegner die Hand zu reichen, verlässt der Boxer den Ring.

Put into German:

6. Don't forget to shut the garage door (—the door of the garage). 7. We must try to reach the top of the hill before midday. 8. Can you do this exercise without using a dictionary? 9. Erwin asks his father to buy him a new bicycle. 10. My alarm-clock begins to ring at quarter past seven.

Have a Try 16

Can you make out a menu for each day of the week? Sort out the various dishes in the list below and put them in the right place in the table!

Hering, Erdbeereis, Erbsensuppe, Schinken, Tomatensuppe, Obst, Hecht, Ananas, Forelle, Leberwurst, Kraftbrühe, Wiener Schnitzel, Garnelen, Gemüsesuppe, Hühnerbraten, Apfelmus, Pfirsiche, Karpfen, Bratwürstchen, Pilzsuppe, Kalbfleisch, Ölsardinen, Fleischbrühe, Schokoladentorte, Rheinsalm, Schildkrötensuppe, Käse, Hammelfleisch.

	Sonntag	Montag	Dienstag	Mittwoch
Suppe				
Fischgericht				
Fleischgericht				
Nachtisch				

	Donnerstag	Freitag	Samstag
Suppe			
Fischgericht			
Fleischgericht			
Nachtisch			

ABOUT "LOOKING". HOW TO SAY "YOURSELF"

One of the words which we use every day is "look". Have you ever thought how many meanings it has? We can *look* through a window, *look* pleased, or *look* for buried treasure, to mention only a few. In German each of these useful ideas is put in a different way.

I *look* in the mirror	is Ich *blicke* (or *sehe*) in den Spiegel
I *look at* the picture	is Ich *sehe* das Bild *an* (NOT an das Bild)
I *look* ill	is Ich *sehe* krank *aus*
Look out!	is *Passen* Sie *auf*!

(Ansehen, aussehen and aufpassen are like aufstehen in Lesson Seven)

I *look for* my handkerchief	is Ich *suche* mein Taschentuch ("FOR" is left out)
He *looks after* his grandmother	is Er *sorgt für* seine Grossmutter

• • • • •

In all languages there are a number of actions you can do *to yourself*. Obviously you can't "chase yourself", but you can very well "hurt, wash or dry yourself".

For "yourself" we need a new word: SICH. Sie waschen sich means "You wash yourself". It could also be "you wash *yourselves*".

In fact sich is a very handy word, for it means in addition *"himself"*, *"herself"*, *"itself"*, *"oneself"* and *"themselves"*.

You can always tell which of these meanings it has by looking at the subject of the verb, thus:

75

er trocknet sich ab,	he dries *him*self
sie wäscht sich,	she washes *her*self
das Kind verletzt sich,	the child hurts *it*self
sie wehren sich,	they defend *them*selves
man setzt sich,	one seats *one*self (sits down)

"*Myself*" and "*ourselves*" are easy; they are simply *mich* and *uns*, which we know already.

In German we really say "I dry *me*" and "we wash *us*"—ich trockne *mich ab* and wir waschen *uns*.

The most interesting thing about SICH is its use with a verb such as "to move".

Let us explain it like this. If someone says to you "Don't move!", you know at once that they don't mean "Don't move the piano!" but "Don't move *yourself*!" In English there is no need to put in the word "yourself", but in German it *must* be there.

This always happens when the action *could* be done to some other thing, but is understood to apply to the subject *itself*.

Some verbs of this kind that you will be sure to need are "FEEL", "OPEN", "BEND" and "STRETCH", as well as "MOVE".

"I feel ill", ich fühle MICH krank. "The door opens", die Tür öffnet SICH. "He bends over the bed", er beugt SICH über das Bett. "The field stretches (extends) as far as the river", das Feld erstreckt SICH bis an den Fluss.

Word List 17

der Hammer, the hammer	anziehen (SICH), to get dressed
der Handschuh, the glove	behaglich, comfortable (of
das Badezimmer, the bathroom	persons)
das Blumenbeet, the flower-bed	fertig, ready
das Raumschiff, the space-ship	überrascht, surprised

(A number of verbs are already given in the text of this Lesson.)

Exercise 17 (*a*)

Put into German:

1. The joiner is looking for his hammer. 2. Don't look so surprised! 3. If you look through the window you can see cars in the street. 4. Tonight I would like to look at a good tele-

vision programme. 5. Mothers look after their children. 6. Suddenly a door in the space-ship opens.

Put into English:

7. Die dichten Wälder erstrecken sich bis an die See. 8. Wenn wir über die Strasse gehen, müssen wir immer gut aufpassen. 9. Im Park beugt sich ein alter Gärtner über ein buntes Blumenbeet. 10. Im November fühle ich mich so behaglich in meinem warmen Bett. 11. Sehen Sie diese schöne Briefmarke an! 12. Der grüne Vorhang bewegt sich im Wind.

Exercise 17 (*b*)

Fill in the missing words and endings. All the *verbs* needed are to be found in the following list (but not in the right order).

essen, suchen, aufstehen, öffnen, anziehen (sich), holen, waschen (sich), trinken, gehen, sitzen.

— Morgen —— ich — sieben —— ——. Dann ——
ich in d— Badezimmer, — mich zu ——. Ich muss
m—— ——, ehe ich mei— Frühstück ——. In d—
Küche —— mei— Frau schon — d— lang— Tisch
und —— eine T—— Kaffee. Wenn ich —— bin, —— ich
mei— Handschuh—. Endlich —— ich die Tür d—
Garage, — mei— alt— Fahrrad zu ——.

Have a Try 17

Ein berühmter Professor in Berlin verbringt (is spending)
einen Abend im Haus eines Freunds. Wenn er nach Hause
zurückkehren will, regnet es stark. Da bittet ihn die Frau
seines Freundes, die Nacht in ihrem Haus zu verbringen, weil
es noch immer so stark regnet. Der Professor dankt ihr und
sagt: „Ich will gern bei Ihnen übernachten".

Plötzlich verschwindet (disappears) der Gast. Man will
gerade zu Bett gehen, wenn der Professor wieder in das
Zimmer kommt, ganz durchnässt (wet through). „Aber um
Himmels willen," sagt sein Freund, „wollten Sie (weren't you
going to) nicht die Nacht hierbleiben, um nicht nass zu
werden?" „Gewiss," antwortet der Professor, „aber ich
musste (had to) schnell nach Hause gehen, um mein Nacht-
hemd zu holen!"

HOW TO SAY "I KNOW". "AS GOOD AS" AND "BETTER THAN"

If you look up "to *know*" in the dictionary you will find two words, WISSEN and KENNEN. One of the commonest mistakes in German is to choose the wrong one.

Here is the best way to distinguish between them. Suppose you want to say:

> "I know that Hund means dog"; "I know what I want"; "I know where (or who) he is"; "I know when the holidays begin"

In all such cases *wissen* must be used, that is, whenever "know" is followed by "*that*", "*what*", "*where*", "*who*", "*when*", "*why*" or any similar word.

Kennen is used only in the sense of "to be familiar with" a thing, person or place. It will be followed by a *noun* or *pronoun*, thus:

> Ich kenne den Arzt: Kennen Sie Paris?: Er kennt mich nicht

Before you try this for yourself, there are just two more things to settle.

First, wissen is one of those "irregular" verbs mentioned in Lesson Two. Its present tense is:

> ich, er, sie, es *WEISS*   wir, Sie, sie *wissen*

As we said, it is really easier than a "regular" verb. It is like muss, müssen in having only two forms.

Second, when was (what), wo (where), wie (how), etc., appear after a verb such as wissen, they behave like conjunctions and the verb in their part of the sentence is placed last:

> Ich weiss, *wo* dieser Vogel sein Nest *hat*

Remember the comma, and notice that all these "joining words" begin with "w".

. . . . .

"As good as" and "better than"

Let us see how to make these two kinds of comparison in German.

1. *AS* good (big, old, etc.) *AS* = *SO* gut (gross, alt, etc.) *WIE*.

Sometimes you will want to put nicht first, e.g. nicht so gut wie . . .

2. small*ER*, deep*ER*, quick*ER* = klein*ER*, tief*ER*, schnell*ER*.

Exactly the same thing is done in English and in German.

THAN is *ALS*. So we can say, for example, Die See ist tief*er als* der Fluss.

It is worth knowing that *all* adjectives in German can have this -ER added, even the long ones, where in English we say, for example, "*more* beautiful", "*more* interesting". The German is interessanter, ungewöhnlicher, and so on.

There is a word for "more" in German: MEHR. But *don't* use it here! Its proper place is before nouns: mehr Geld, mehr Brot, etc.

Finally, learn the word BESSER (= "better") and notice a little trick with adjectives of one syllable containing "a", "o" or "u":

"older", "bigger" and "younger" are *älter*, *grösser* and *jünger*

i.e. ·· is added along with the -er.

Word List 18

der Pfarrer, the parson	die Meile, the mile
der Tourist, the tourist	stumpf, blunt
(pl. -en)	süss, sweet
der Zahnarzt, the dentist	vielleicht, perhaps

Exercise 18 (a)

Put into German:

1. Do you know a good dentist? 2. The parson knows what the organist is going to play on Sunday. 3. These tourists would like to know whether (ob) they may take photos in the church. 4. We always eat at this hotel, because my family knows the waiter. 5. Ask that policeman; perhaps he will know where the famous bridge is (liegt). 6. Do the passengers know that* this train leaves (abfahren) five minutes earlier on Saturday?

Put into English:

7. Jedes Kind weiss, dass ein Berg höher als ein Hügel ist. 8. Ein Flugzeug fährt schneller als ein Zug. 9. Mein Bett ist bequemer als dieser Stuhl. 10. Ein Bleistift ist nicht so nützlich wie ein Kugelschreiber.

Exercise 18 (b)

Complete the following sentences:

Example: Der Sommer ist *wärmer als der Winter*

1. Ein reifer Apfel ist —— —— ein grüner Apfel. 2. Ein scharfes Taschenmesser ist besser als —— —— ——. 3. Ein neuer Teppich ist —— —— ein alter Teppich. 4. Ein Hund ist nicht —— —— —— ein Pferd. 5. Eine Stadt hat —— Häuser —— ein Dorf. 6. Ein Café ist —— —— ein Hotel. 7. Elektrisches Licht ist —— —— Gaslicht.

Put into German:

8. This alarm-clock is more reliable than my watch. 9. This book is not as thick as a dictionary. 10. London is bigger than

* N.B. in this sense "that" is always *dass*.

Berlin. 11. A mile is longer than a kilometre. 12. That girl is not as pretty as her sister.

Exercise 18 (*c*)

kalt   (nicht) so kalt wie   kälter als

For practice, do this aloud with all the adjectives you have learned so far.

Have a Try 18

An einem dunklen Abend machen drei Studenten eine Reise nach Bonn. Plötzlich kommen sie an einen Kreuzweg und wissen nun nicht, ob sie nach rechts oder nach links gehen sollen.

Bald entdeckt (discovers) einer der Studenten einen Wegweiser mit drei Armen. Weil es aber so dunkel ist, kann keiner lesen, was darauf steht. Also steigt der erste auf die Schultern des zweiten und zündet ein Streichholz an, aber der

Wind löscht es sofort aus. Dann versucht sein Freund, die Buchstaben (letters) zu lesen, aber ihm ergeht es nicht besser.

Endlich steigt der dritte hinauf, bricht die drei Arme ab und springt wieder zur Erde. Jetzt können sie wohl die Aufschrift „Bonn" lesen, aber auf welchen Weg sie zeigen sollte (should), weiss keiner!

LESSON NINETEEN

ANOTHER NEW SENTENCE-PATTERN ("WHO"
AND "WHICH"). "ZU + INFINITIVE" AGAIN.
USING "WHO" AND "WHICH"

Look at these two sentences:

Here sits a boy.   The boy has big ears.

These two remarks would obviously be better expressed in
one sentence. But this time we can't simply join them with
"because", "when", or any similar word (except "and",
which would sound very feeble!)

The linking can best be done by putting the word "WHO"
instead of "the boy" in the second sentence, thus:

Here sits a boy *who* has big ears.

If we are talking about *things*, "WHICH" is used instead of
"who":

I have a guitar *which* I am learning to play.

In German there is no difference between "who" and
"which". If we are referring to a *der* word—person *or* thing—
"who" and "which" are both *DER*.

Examples: Ein Junge, *der* ...   (A boy *who* ...)
            Der Garten, *der* ...   (The garden *which* ...)

As you may have guessed, *DIE* and *DAS* will be our words
for both "who" and "which" if the noun referred to is a die or
das word:

Eine Gitarre, *die* ...   Das Haus, *das* ...

Yes, these words are exactly the same as the words for "the",
but you won't get the meanings confused.

If we look at some complete sentences including the new

{ der
{ die, we shall find they produce two very important patterns.
{ das

The sentence we began with is a good example of the first:

Hier sitzt ein Junge, *der* grosse Ohren *hat*

The word for "who" or "which" sends the verb to the end of its own part exactly like wenn, weil, etc., and this part is marked off by a comma.* The "who" or "which" part forms the *second half* of the sentence.

For the second pattern let us take this example:

Der Baum ist hoch. Der Baum wächst in meinem Garten.

Using der, we get: Der Baum, *der* in meinem Garten *wächst*, ist hoch. Again, der has its verb last, but the "which" clause is placed *inside* the other sentence.

Learn these two kinds of sentence and be ready to practise them in the Exercises which follow.

. . . . .

Can we go back to "zu + infinitive" for a moment? Suppose the "infinitive" is a verb such as aufstehen or ansehen (Lesson Seven)?

This is what happens:

Ich versuche immer, früh auf*zu*stehen
Ich besuche das Aquarium, um (mir) die Fische an*zu*sehen

The "zu" goes *between* the extra word and the verb itself, and the whole thing is written as *one* word.

Word List 19

der Schaffner, the conductor	aufflammen, to blaze up
gefährlich, dangerous	heissen, to be called
eben, just	(ich heisse, I "am called")

* If there are *two* verbs in this part, the "can", "will" type of verb is placed last again:

. . . , *weil* ich ein Speiseeis essen *möchte*.
der Junge, *der* ein Speiseeis essen *möchte*.

Exercise 19 (a)

Join with the correct word for "who" or "which"—and watch the pattern:

1. Ein Pferd ist ein Tier. Ein Pferd zieht einen Wagen.
2. Die Schere ist stumpf. Meine Frau holt die Schere aus ihrem Nähkasten.
3. Ich habe ein schönes Auto. Das Auto fährt schnell auf der Autobahn.
4. Der Kühlschrank steht in unserer Küche. Der Kühlschrank ist neu.
5. Das Fahrrad kostet 100 Mark. Ich möchte das Fahrrad mit meinem Taschengeld kaufen.

Put into German:

6. The man who gives us our tickets on (in) the bus is called the conductor.
7. Please pass me the glass which is on the sideboard.
8. A knife which is too (zu) sharp can be dangerous.
9. A joiner is a man who makes tables and chairs.
10. The boy who lives next door is trying to make a model aeroplane.

Exercise 19 (b)

Put into German:

1. When the old professor goes to bed, he forgets to take his shoes off. 2. You mustn't try to get into a bus when it is moving. 3. The fire is just beginning to blaze up. 4. I am

going into my bedroom in order to get dressed. 5. Ask Erich
to switch on the radio.

Answer in German, using a word for "who" or "which":

6. Was ist ein Fahrgast? 7. Was ist ein Matrose? 8. Was ist
ein Wecker?

Complete:

9. Im Garten liegt ein Hund, der . . . . 10. Ich muss
die Milch trinken, d— meine Schwester in d— Glas
gie——.

Have a Try 19

In Deutschland hat fast jede Stadt ein Theater. Grosse
Städte haben auch ein Opernhaus, wo man Opern aufführt.
Wenn wir ins Theater eintreten, lassen wir unseren Überzieher,
Hut oder Regenschirm in der Garderobe und gehen dann in
den Zuschauerraum. Vor uns ist die Bühne, wo die Schau-
spieler auftreten. Wir haben Parkettplätze; über uns sind die
Logen und Galerien. Wenn alles bereit ist, muss man den
Vorhang aufziehen, den man nach jedem Akt wieder herablässt.
Wir kaufen ein Programm und warten, bis die Vorstellung
beginnt.

"WHO" AND "WHICH" (CONTINUED). HOW TO SAY "I WAIT FOR"

Here are a few more necessary facts about "who" and "which".

1. Ich kenne ein*en* Schüler, *der* Mathematik gern hat.
   Er wohnt in ein*em* Haus, *das* keine Garage hat.
   Helga ist die Tochter *der* Frau, *die* im Laden arbeitet.

From these sentences you can see that any "changed" ending (italicized) in the *first* part does not affect the word for "who" or "which". This is based on the *original* der, die or das of the noun just in front of it.

2. Die Äpfel, *die* wir im Obstgarten pflücken, sind süss.

DIE is "who" or "which" referring back to a *plural* noun.

3.   There are two ways in which the actual der, die or das can be changed. When this happens, they change exactly like the words for "the", i.e. to de*n*, de*m*, etc.

(*a*) Look at the following examples:

> Ein Gärtner, *der* mich kennt
> Ein Gärtner, *den ich* kenne
> Der Brief, *den mein* Bruder liest

When "who*m*" or "which" is the *object* of the verb in its *own part*, der becomes *den*. Die and das of course would not change.

With a masculine *person* the change to "*whom*" in English is your clue. An even better tip is to watch for the extra subject (ich and mein Bruder).

(*b*) The other change comes when "who" or "which" follows a *preposition*, e.g. "with which", "for whom".
Examples:

> Der Ball, *mit dem* ich spiele
> Die Garage, *in der* das Auto steht
> Der Wald, *durch den* wir wandern

NEVER try to say in German "The chair *which* he is sitting *on*" or "The pen *which* I write *with*". You must always turn these into the form ". . . *on which* he is sitting"; ". . . *with which* I write".

4. Notice that the words for "who" or "which" can never be left out in German. In English we can say "A man I know", "The book I am reading". In German these *must* be Ein Mann, *den* ich kenne and Das Buch, *das* ich lese.

Finally, there is our English habit of using "that" as an alternative to "who" or "which", e.g. "A tree that grows". NEVER put *dass* in this case. Whenever "that" means "who" or "which", it *must* be der, die, das, etc.

How to say "I wait for the bus"

"Wait" is one of a number of verbs which we always use along with a certain preposition. We just *know*, from habit, that we wait FOR things, not "at" or "to" them. Similarly we *ask FOR*, think OF (or ABOUT), and are afraid OF a thing.

The same kind of construction is used in German, except that the preposition is not always the one you would expect. For example, to "wait for" is warten *AUF*, not für. Then, of course, we have to think what *ending* the German preposition will produce on the word which follows it.

This is what happens in the case of the four verbs mentioned so far:

"wait for", warten AUF (List 1 type, with "object" endings)
"think of", denken AN (List 1 type, with "object" endings)
"ask for", bitten UM (List 1 type, with "object" endings)
"be afraid of", fürchten SICH VOR (List 2 type endings).

Examples:

> Ich warte auf *den* Autobus
> Ich denke an *meine* Mutter
> Ich bitte um *das* Brot
> Fürchten Sie sich vor *diesem* Hund?

The material in this Lesson, you will notice, provides some useful revision of the endings you have learned in previous chapters.

Word List 20

der Hausflur, the vestibule	denken, to think
die Maus, the mouse	fürchten (sich), to be afraid
das Gebäude, the building	füttern, to feed
das Loch, the hole	interessieren (sich) FÜR, to be
Doktor, doctor (as title)	interested IN
	predigen, to preach

Exercise 20 (a)

Join with a word for "who" or "which" and find the correct pattern:

1. Das Haus hat sieben Zimmer. Ich wohne in dem Haus.
2. Der Tisch steht in der Mitte des Zimmers. Ich sitze an dem Tisch.
3. Der Zug fährt um halb zwei ab. Ich warte jetzt auf den Zug.
4. Auf dem Zaun sitzt ein brauner Vogel. Ich füttere den Vogel.
5. Ich suche meine Füllfeder. Ich will einen Brief mit der Füllfeder schreiben.
6. Die Maus kommt aus einem kleinen Loch. Das Loch ist neben der Tür.

Put into English:

7. Interessiert sich Ihr Freund für Briefmarken? 8. Dieses Mädchen fürchtet sich nicht vor einer kleinen Maus. 9. In dem Kleiderschrank, der auf dem Hausflur steht, hängt meine alte Jacke. 10. In dem Eimer, den ich in der Küche sehe, ist

schmutziges Wasser. 11. Heute morgen müssen wir lange auf den Briefträger warten. 12. Ich denke immer an die Einkäufe, die ich am Montag in der Stadt machen muss.

Exercise 20 (b)

Put into German:

1. I don't like to wait for my breakfast. 2. Do you know the parson who is preaching at our church on Sunday? (put *time* before *place*). 3. The scent of the flowers which my mother is gathering is very strong. 4. I know no doctor who is more famous than Dr. Weiss. 5. Every organist must be interested in music. 6. What is that song called that you are singing? 7. The coffee we are drinking is nearly cold.

Complete:

8. Der Zug, —— d— ich warte, kommt in zehn Minuten ——.

9. Das Pferd, d— auf dies— Feld arbeitet, s—ht müde ——.

10. Das grosse Gebäude, vor d— das Auto steht, ...
11. Ich habe einen guten Schläger, mit d— ich . . . .
12. Aus dem Briefkasten, der . . . . , ...

Have a Try 20

Wir wohnen im Zentrum der Stadt an den Grünanlagen, die den inneren Stadtteil umschliessen. Besonders unseren Palmengarten möchte ich kurz schildern. Zwischen Rasen und Blumenbeeten liegen die Gartenhäuser. In der tropischen Luft gedeihen seltene afrikanische Pflanzen und Blumen, die einen eigenartigen süssen Duft ausströmen. Auf Goldfisch-teichen blühen Wasserrosen und Algen. Da zeigen sich auch fleischfressende Pflanzen. Das schönste ist wohl das Palmen-haus. Mächtige Palmen erheben sich von den Erdbeeten, wo eine muntere Quelle sich schlängelt, um sich zuletzt in einen Wasserfall aufzulösen.

HOW TO SAY "HAVE YOU ASKED?" HOW TO SAY "LAST WEEK"

In Lesson Five we learned how to make better use of our verbs by introducing kann, muss, will, etc. These, we know, go along with the *infinitive* of any verb.

We can do something equally useful with "*has*" and "*have*": think how often somebody says to you "Have you washed your hands?" or "Have you brushed your teeth?"

Whereas "can" and "must" are followed by an infinitive ("can *wash*", "must *brush*"), "have" is followed by a new word "WASH*ED*" or "BRUSH*ED*".

English, too, has its "endings", and the ending -ED can be put on lots of words, e.g. "I have play*ed*, sav*ed*, ask*ed*".

Let us see what this would be in German. (We already know "has" and "have".)

> Have you asked?—Haben Sie GEfragT?
> He has saved   —Er hat GEsparT
> We have played —Wir haben GEspielT
> I have brushed —Ich habe GEbürsteT

In these examples the word to put with any part of "to have" is

GE (stem of verb) *T*

(German -T matches the English -ED: a long time ago the English words "played", "saved", etc. also had a "GE-" in front corresponding to the German GE-.)

Sometimes, instead of ending in -ED, the English words following "has" and "have" end in -*EN*. We say, for example, "I have giv*EN*, brok*EN*, writt*EN*".

The German word in these cases is even closer to the English:

93

I have given —Ich habe GEgebEN
Have you broken?—Haben Sie GEbrochEN?
He has written —Er hat GEschriebEN
They have seen —Sie haben GEsehEN

Our new word is

GE (stem of verb) EN

(sometimes with spelling-change).

We shall leave the question of this spelling-change until later and finish this section with three useful notes:

1. GEspielT and GEsehEN are called in grammar-books the PAST PARTICIPLES of the verbs spielen and sehen. You may find this "technical term" convenient when referring to them.

2. Verbs with past participles ending in -T are called "WEAK" verbs and those whose past participles end in -EN are called "STRONG" verbs.

This doesn't mean that some verbs are "stronger" or better than others! It is just a neat way of distinguishing between them, and you will find the abbreviation (W)—for weak—used in later Word Lists and in the Alphabetical List at the end of the book.

3. In longer sentences the past participle, like the infinitive, normally comes at the *end*:

Der junge Hans *muss* seine Aufgaben vor dem Abendessen *machen*.
Der junge Hans *hat* seine Aufgaben vor dem Abendessen *gemacht*.

Wollen Sie diesem Vogel ein Stück Brot *geben*?
Haben Sie diesem Vogel ein Stück Brot *gegeben*?

The part of haben always takes the place of the will, kann type of verb, i.e. *next* after a phrase or adverb and *last* after a conjunction, "who" or "which".

Examples:

In der Kirche *darf* ich nicht *rauchen*
In der Kirche *habe* ich nicht *geraucht*

..., obgleich ich den Arzt *fragen muss*
..., obgleich ich den Arzt *gefragt habe*

der Junge, der meine Briefmarken *sehen will*
der Junge, der meine Briefmarken *gesehen hat*

. . . . .

How to say "Last week"

There are a number of time-expressions such as "last week", "next Friday", "every year", or "every morning" which we often put at the beginning of sentences.

In German all these must be given "object" endings (Lesson Three). Only der words, of course, will be affected, but it so happens that most of the "time" words (day, month, morning, evening, etc.) are in fact der words.

"Last" is vorig or letzt : "next" is nächst

So we get, for example:

Vorig*en* Montag
Jed*en* Abend   *but*   Nächst*e* Woche   Jed*es* } Jahr
Jed*en* Morgen   Jed*e* Stunde   Nächst*es* }

(*N.B.* "one day" is usually put as ein*es* Tag*es*).

Word List 21

der Abend, the evening	geklebt, stuck
der Koffer, the trunk	gelassen, left
der Umschlag, the envelope	geleert, emptied
die Zeitschrift, the magazine	gelesen, read
je, ever	geschenkt, given (presented)
nie, never	gespart, saved
gefunden, found	gestrickt, knitted
gegeben, given	gesucht, looked for
gegossen, poured	getanzt, danced
gejagt, chased	getrocknet, dried
gekauft, bought	getrunken, drunk
	gezeigt, showed

(Notice that some English past participles are irregular.)

Exercise 21 (a)

Put into English:

1. Haben Sie den Film gesehen, den man diese Woche in unserem Kino zeigt? 2. Ich muss das neue Radio hören, das

mein Freund heute gekauft hat. 3. Fragen Sie den Gepäckträger, wo er den grossen Koffer gelassen hat! 4. Ich habe
meine Fahrkarte überall gesucht. 5. Wo ist die Zeitschrift, die
ich im Bett gelesen habe? 6. Was hat Frau Schmidt ihrer
Tochter zum Geburtstag geschenkt?

Rewrite these sentences, changing the italicized verbs into
hat ge——:

7. Karl *zeigt* mir ein schönes Bild, das er in einem alten Buch
findet.

8. In der Küche *leert* die Putzfrau ihren Eimer.

9. Das Kind *trinkt* die Milch, die seine Mutter in ein Glas
giesst.

10. Hans *spart* sein Geld, um einen neuen Kugelschreiber
zu kaufen.

Exercise 21 (*b*)

Put into German:

1. Have you ever danced with that girl? 2. My wife has
knitted a green pullover. 3. Next week I would like to meet

your sister. 4. Every morning I sleep until 7 o'clock. 5. Next
year we are going to Frankfurt, where my uncle has bought a
house. 6. After I have dried myself, I am going to put on a new
shirt. 7. Every evening my friend comes home at 6.30. 8.
Have you stuck a stamp on this envelope? 9. What has your
sister bought in that shop? 10. My dog has never chased a cat.

Have a Try 21

Some German riddles

1. Was hört ohne Ohren, spricht ohne Mund und antwortet
in allen Sprachen?
2. Es geht durchs ganze Land und bleibt immer da, wo es ist.
3. Es hat einen Rücken und kann nicht liegen,
   es hat zwei Flügel und kann nicht fliegen.
   Es hat ein Bein und kann nicht stehen,
   es kann laufen und kann nicht gehen.
4. Wer hat es bequemer, Kaffee oder Tee?
5. Es geht durchs Fenster und zerbricht es nicht.

HOW TO SAY "I HAVE GONE". HOW TO SAY "THE GREATEST"

Sometimes—usually in poetry—we read "The night *is* gone" or "we *are* come", where we would usually say "*has* gone" and "*have* come".

In German there are a few verbs which *always* work like this, even in everyday speech. Instead of habe, hat and haben, they must have BIN, IST and SIND with their past participles. And they are in such frequent use that we must add them to those learned in Lesson Twenty-one.

These verbs are practically all ways of *moving*, that is, ways of getting *from one place to another*. The commonest are gehen, kommen and fahren, then come laufen, steigen, fliegen and springen (jump).

Fallen must be included; although falling is not exactly a way of travelling, it is after all the quickest way of getting, say, from a tree to the ground!

Finally aufstehen (to get up) and einschlafen (to go to sleep) come into this list, because they are "movements" from one *position* or *state* to another.

So we must be ready for

> ich *bin* gekommen (I *have* come)
> er *ist* gelaufen (he *has* run)
> wir *sind* gefallen (we *have* fallen)
> and so on.

·　　·　　·　　·　　·

Here are two more things we must know about past participles:

1. The past participles of verbs such as *an*kommen and *ein*schlafen are an*GE*kommen, ein*GE*schlafen, etc. (Compare this with an*zu*sehen and auf*zu*stehen in Lesson Nineteen.)

2. Suppose we are using a verb such as besuchen (to visit) or verschwinden. The full form would sound so clumsy that the GE- is omitted.

> I have visited, ich habe besucht
> it has disappeared, es ist verschwunden

This happens whenever a verb begins with BE- or VER-, and also ER-, GE-, ZER- EMP- and ENT-. You need not learn all these now, but the list is given for reference.

. . . . .

How to say "the greatest"

In Lesson Eighteen we learned the words for "bigger", "younger", etc. Let us go a step further and deal with "greatest", "youngest" and "smallest".

In English we add -EST to the adjective. In German we add -*ST* (and ·· on a, o, and u in words of one syllable).

> kleinST, smallest   schnellST, fastest   jüngST, youngest
> höchST, highest

-EST is needed in German only when an adjective ends in a letter such as -*t* or -*z* and would be unpronounceable without the extra -E:

> kürzEst, shortest   ältEst, oldest

GRÖSS*T*, greatest, biggest (from gross) and *BEST*, best (from gut) are irregular and should be learned separately.

You will remember (Lesson Eighteen) that "more interesting" was interessant*er*. Similarly, interessant*EST* will be "*most* interesting", berühmtEST, "*most* famous", and so on.

These words can be used in two ways. Before *nouns* they need the normal adjective endings on top of the -ST:

> Examples: die grösstE Stadt mein ältestER Bruder
> in dem kleinstEN Dorf

With *verbs*, they are used in a special way:

he *runs* fastest, er läuft AM schnellstEN
who *writes* best?, wer schreibt AM bestEN?
the days *are* (at their) longest in summer, im Sommer sind die
Tage AM längstEN

Word List 22

der Liegestuhl, the deck-chair	past participle of:
der Metzger, the butcher	fahren, gefahren
der Aufsatz, the essay	fallen, gefallen
der Salon, the drawing-room	fliegen, geflogen
die Klasse, the class	gehen, gegangen
die Reise, the journey	graben, gegraben
die Sperre, the barrier	kommen, gekommen
das Rindfleisch, the beef	laufen, gelaufen
nett, nice	schreiben, geschrieben
abholen, to meet (at stations, etc.)	spielen, gespielt
verkaufen (W), to sell	springen, gesprungen
umgraben, to dig over	stehen, gestanden
scheinen, to shine	warten, gewartet
steigen, to climb	

Exercise 22 (a)

Rewrite with the verbs changed to $\left.\begin{array}{l}\text{ist}\\\text{hat}\end{array}\right\}$ + $\dfrac{\text{past}}{\text{participle}}$:

1. Dieser Zug *fährt* von Köln nach Frankfurt. 2. *Steht* mein Bruder schon auf? 3. *Verkauft* der Metzger das Stück Rindfleisch, das ich im Laden *sehe*? 4. Ein schwarzer Vogel *fliegt* über unser Haus. 5. Die Maus *läuft* in ihr Loch, weil unsere Katze vom Stuhl *springt*.

Put into English:

6. Renate ist das netteste Mädchen, mit dem ich je getanzt habe. 7. Ich habe oft versucht, über diese Mauer zu steigen. 8. Wer hat Ihnen jenen langen Brief geschickt? 9. Wenn der Gärtner die Blumenbeete umgegraben hat, wird er die letzten Rosen pflücken. 10. Obgleich das rote Auto um die Ecke verschwunden ist, kann ich es noch hören.

Exercise 22 (b)

Put into German:

1. An apple has fallen from the tree under which Mr. Brown is sitting. 2. Two birds have flown out of the tree, because Mr. Brown has got up from his deck-chair. 3. Has the train from

(aus) Hamburg arrived? I have promised to meet my sister at the barrier. 4. The doctor lives in the biggest house in the village. 5. I have waited (the) longest. 6. This light shines (the) brightest. 7. Although Karl is the smallest boy in the class, he has written the best essay.

Complete:

8. H—— Sie mei— Mütze geseh—? Ich h—— sie überall gesuch—. 9. Nach—— wir die Einkäufe gem—— h——, k—— wir eine Weile i— Park sitz—. 10. Heute

h— mei——Schwester i— Salon Klavier gesp——. 11.
Jen— Pfarrer h—— mit d— Arzt gespr——. 12. Ist eine
Luftreise gefährlich— —— eine Reise mit d— Zug?

Have a Try 22

Nahe bei Frankfurt liegt der schöne und waldreiche Taunus,
vielleicht das schönste Gebirge Deutschlands und ein beliebtes
Reiseziel der Frankfurter. Gepflegte Spazierwege führen den
Besucher auf die schönsten Aussichtsplätze. Fast auf allen
Höhen der einzelnen Berge sind Gasthäuser oder Aussichts-
plätze, die einen herrlichen Blick in die Tiefebene bieten.

Der höchste Berg im Taunus ist der Grosse Feldberg, 881 m
hoch. Von hier hat man die schönste Aussicht im ganzen
Taunus. Der Feldberg bildet ein Plateau, auf dem drei
Gasthäuser und ein Aussichtsturm stehen.

Der zweithöchste Berg im Taunus ist der Altkönig. Dann
folgt der Kleine Feldberg, auf dem ein Observatorium für
Erdbebenmessung steht.

LESSON TWENTY-THREE

ABOUT WORDS ENDING IN -ING

Words ending in -ING occur very frequently in everyday English. In German there are several ways of rendering them:

1. When we speak of "the flying Dutchman", "running water" or "a wandering minstrel", the words *"flying"*, *"running"* and *"wandering"* are really adjectives, although they are made from the verbs "to fly", "to run", etc.

In German such words are made by adding *-D* to the *infinitive*. They will of course need the right adjective ending as well. So we get:

> der fliegen*de* Holländer : fliessen*des* Wasser : ein wandern*der* Spielmann

2. Words such as "reading", "writing" and "swimming" can be *nouns*, e.g. "Swimming is a great sport", "Reading is my hobby". In German, these nouns are simply the infinitive written with a capital letter. All such nouns are das words, although the das is often left out.

Examples:

> Lesen und Schreiben; *das B*ellen der Hunde

3. When we say *"Having* no friends, I stay at home" or *"Finding* no one at home, I went away again", we really mean *"Because* I have" and *"Because* I found".

In German, put *Weil* ich keine Freunde habe, . . . and so on.

4. There is a special use with *"see"* and *"hear"*, e.g. "I hear the wind *howling"*, "I see him *running"*.

This is done in German with the *infinitive*, thus:

> Ich höre den Wind *heulen*; Ich sehe ihn *laufen*

5. After some *nouns* we have another special use of -ing:

"The *hope of finding* gold"; "The *pleasure of meeting* you"

In German, we bring in once again "ZU + infinitive":

Die Hoffnung, Gold *zu finden*: Das Vergnügen, Sie *zu treffen*

6. The nouns in paragraph 2 above are all "actions". There is another kind of noun ending in -ing where no action is indicated, for example "An *opening* in the wall".

The corresponding noun in German ends in -UNG, and all such nouns are die words: Eine Öffn*ung* in der Mauer.

It is worth noting that German words ending in -ung often match English words ending in -TION or -MENT, as well as -ing.

For instance, die Mess*ung*, "the measure*ment*": eine Samml*ung*, "a collec*tion*".

7. REMEMBER that sometimes -ing in English verbs has NO equivalent at all in German:

"I *am* com*ing*", "*Is* he com*ing*?" and the like are simply "Ich komme", "Kommt er?", etc.

("Was coming" and "were coming"—when we learn them—will turn out to be the same as "came".)

"I have *been* writ*ing*, play*ing*", etc., are translated simply as "I have written, played", etc.

Word List 23

der Ausflug, the trip, excursion	das Vergnügen, the pleasure
der Schuster, the cobbler	ausfindig machen (W), to find out
die Fahrt, the journey, voyage	beantworten (W), to answer
die Ausstellung, the exhibition	zwitschern (W), to twitter
die Hoffnung, the hope	modern, modern
das Blatt, the leaf	

Exercise 23 (a)

Put into English:

1. Ich habe keine Hoffnung, nächstes Jahr eine Fahrt im Raumschiff zu machen. 2. Ein schneidender Wind treibt die

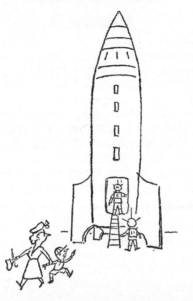

Blätter auf die Strasse. 3. In jenem Haus kann ich ein Kind singen hören. 4. Das Rasseln meines Weckers ist heute morgen sehr laut. 5. Ein schlafender Hund liegt auf meinem Bett. 6. Am Sonntag werden wir das Vergnügen haben, einen Ausflug auf das Land zu machen. 7. Heute habe ich eine schöne Erzählung in der Zeitschrift gelesen.

Put into German:

8. What are you putting in your pocket? 9. Have the passengers been asking from (say "on") which platform the train starts? 10. May I have the pleasure of dancing with your sister? 11. Do you see the fire blazing up? 12. The policeman gets into a waiting car. 13. I like to hear the twittering of the birds in my garden. 14. Having no key, I can't open this door.

Exercise 23 (b)

Complete:

Es ist Sonnabend. —— —— nach sieben —— ich aus d—
Bett. Nachdem ich m—— Frühstück ge—— h——, —— ich
d— Brief von Onkel Heinrich be————. Dann —— ich zwei
Paar Schuh— vom —— abholen. W—— ich in d— Stadt
bin, m—— ich d— neu— Ausstellung modern—
Fernsehapparate n—— d— Rathaus besuch——. Viel——
w—— ich d— Vergnügen haben, Freund— zu treff——
und mit —— ein— Tasse Kaffee i— Café — trink——.
—— ich wieder —— Haus komme, muss ich —— Bahnhof
d— Z–g– für unser— Ausflug — Sonntag ausfindig mach——.

Have a Try 23

Nun sind wir schon vierzehn Tage am Meer, und es gefällt
uns sehr gut. Gleich am ersten Morgen sind wir früh
aufgestanden, um einen Sonnenaufgang am Meer zu erleben.
Wie ein Feuerball steigt die Sonne aus dem Wasser, das
glitzernd vor uns liegt.

Wasser, Wind und Sonne locken uns täglich hinaus. Ich
schwimme viel, während Gisela sich lieber im Sand oder im
Strandkorb beschäftigt. Wir haben schon herrliche Dünen-
wanderungen gemacht; auch einen Überseedampfer haben wir
eingehend besichtigt.

HOW TO BE POLITE IN GERMAN. MORE ABOUT GESCHRIEBEN AND GEFLOGEN

In shops, at the station, in the train or the street, for example, one often needs to approach a person with a question or a request of some kind. In German, the important thing is to know how to begin.

Here are some correct "openings" for most situations. Learn them and see if you can use them in the Exercise below:

In shops	Ich möchte gern . . . haben.
	Darf ich Sie bitten, mir . . . zu {geben ? / zeigen ?
Asking a favour, permission, etc.	Stört es Sie, wenn ich . . . ? (Do you mind if . . . ?)
	Würden Sie so freundlich sein, mir . . . zu ——en ? (Would you be kind enough to . . . ?)
Asking for information, etc.	Können Sie mir bitte helfen ?
	Können Sie mir bitte sagen, wo (wie) (wann) (= when) . . . ?

. . . . .

One more point about words ending in -ing. In the previous Have a Try piece, did you notice Das Wasser *liegt glitzernd* ? In addition to their use as adjectives, German words ending in -d, such as blendend (dazzling) and weinend (weeping) are frequently used with *verbs*.

Examples: Die Sonne scheint blenden*d* auf den Schnee
Das Kind läuft weinen*d* zu seiner Mutter

There is one odd exception. "He comes running" or "A bird comes flying" are Er kommt GELAUFEN and Ein Vogel kommt GEFLOGEN, i.e. the *past participle* takes the place of laufend and fliegend.

This happens ONLY with "TO COME" + a verb of "MOVEMENT".

. . . . .

In Lesson Twenty-one we noticed that words such as geschri*e*ben, gefl*o*gen and gespr*o*chen (the past participles of "strong" verbs), often contain a vowel different from that in the original stem (schr*ei*b-, fl*ie*g-, spr*e*ch-).

At this stage we had better learn how the new vowel is decided. If we know the vowel in the *infinitive*, we can in fact always predict how the past participle will be spelt, except in the case of a few irregular verbs. The IE in fliegen obviously becomes O in geflogen, therefore we can say that all other strong verbs with IE in the infinitive will make a similar change, e.g. schl*ie*ssen—geschl*o*ssen.

The connection between the vowels in the infinitive and past participle is shown in the following table. Learn *one* example of each type and you will automatically know the rest:

Infinitive	*Past Participle*
E	O or E
(spr*e*chen)	(gespr*o*chen)
(g*e*ben)	(geg*e*ben)
IE	O
(fl*ie*gen)	(gefl*o*gen)
I	U
(tr*i*nken)	(getr*u*nken)
(f*i*nden)	(gef*u*nden)
A	A
(f*a*llen)	(gef*a*llen)
(f*a*hren)	(gef*a*hren)
EI	IE
(schr*ei*ben)	(geschr*ie*ben)

Finally, for reference, here are a few of the commonest *irregular* past participles:

gegangen (from gehen)	*gekommen* (from kommen)
gebracht (from bringen)	*gewusst* (from wissen)
gesessen (from sitzen)	*geschnitten* (from schneiden)

Word List 24

der Hundertmarkschein, the 100-mark note	erklären(W), to explain
der Weg, the way	wechseln(W), to change
die Anzeige, the notice	(money, etc.)
die Haltestelle, the bus-stop	
das Konzert, the concert	

Exercise 24 (a)

Write the questions you would ask in German on the following occasions:

1. Sie wollen eine Uhr kaufen, die Sie im Schaufenster gesehen haben.
2. Sie wollen den Weg zum Bahnhof wissen.
3. Sie wollen im Zug das Fenster offen haben.

4. Sie wollen wissen, wann das Konzert beginnt.
5. Sie wollen einen Hundertmarkschein wechseln.
6. Sie wollen zwei Apfelsinen kaufen.

Put into German:

7. Do you mind if I switch the wireless on? 8. Can you please tell me where the bus-stop is? 9. Would you be kind enough to explain this notice to me? 10. May I ask you to speak more slowly?

Exercise 24 (b)

1. Write the past participle, with er hat or er ist, of each verb in the following list:

halten, singen, lesen, steigen, sprechen, wachsen, kriechen, gehen, treiben, fangen, zerbrechen, kommen, bringen, riechen, sehen.

(Examples: er hat geschrieben, er ist gelaufen. All these verbs are "strong" or "irregular".)

Put into English:

2. Können Sie mir bitte sagen, wieviel diese braunen Schuhe kosten? 3. Würden Sie so freundlich sein, mir das Brot zu reichen? 4. Weil heute schulfrei ist, sind die Jungen singend auf das Land gefahren. 5. Mein kleiner Hund kommt bellend ins Zimmer gesprungen.

Complete:

6. K—— Sie m— b—— sagen, in welch— Richtung d— Gross— Feldberg lie—? 7. W—— Sie so freund—— s——, d— Butter aus d— Kühlschrank zu h——? 8. St—— es Sie, wenn ich i— nächst— Zimmer Klavier spiel—? 9. Ich h—— ei— schön— Briefmarke auf dies— Brief gek——. 10. Ei— Fahrgast d—— nicht verg——en, sei— Fahrkarte vor d— Reise zu l——.

Have a Try 24

„Aufstehen, Toni!" Mitleidig lächelnd beugt sich die Mutter über den Schläfer. Sie fährt mit der Hand über die braunen Haare.

„Aufstehen, Toni. Es ist Zeit!" Die alte Pendeluhr schlägt zögernd und misstönig sechsmal. Die Mutter ist wieder in die Küche gegangen. Fröstelnd beginnt Toni sich anzukleiden. Tausend Gedanken schwirren ihm durch den Kopf. Dann geht auch er in die Küche, um sich zu waschen. Die Mutter hat das Wasser heute gewärmt. Und während er später schlürfend den heissen Kaffee trinkt, sieht er nicht, wie die Mutter eine grosse, glitzernde Träne aus den Augen wischt. Heute geht der Junge zum erstenmal in die Fabrik. Und ihr grosses liebendes Herz sträubt sich dagegen.

HOW TO SAY "UP", "DOWN" AND "ALONG".
HOW TO SAY "WHOSE"

If a person comes up the stairs, and you are already at the top, you will see him coming die Treppe *her*auf. If he then stands at the top, whilst you go down, *he* will see *you* going die Treppe *hin*unter.

These little words hin and her are a very important feature of German.

Hin really means "*away from* here" and her means "*towards* here", but they are usually combined with other words such as auf, unter and aus and are not translated separately.

Thus die Treppe *her*auf means "up the stairs", with "towards here" or "towards me" understood. Die Treppe *hin*auf would also mean "up the stairs", but suggesting "*away* up the stairs", leaving me at the bottom.

If you think a minute this will soon become clear. Here are two more examples that might help. When you are sitting in a room and someone knocks, you call *Her*ein! ("Come in!"), but if you throw something out of the window, it will go *hin*aus.

The words for "up" and "down" form some very useful phrases, for example:

> *die* Strasse hinauf (or herauf), up the street
> *das* Rheintal herauf (hinunter, etc.), up (down) the Rhine valley
> *den* Hügel hinauf (herunter, etc.), up or down the hill

(Notice that the nouns are written with "object" endings.) The only other word which is used in this way is entlang (= "along").

Examples: die Allee ⎱
das Ufer ⎰entlang   along ⎰ the avenue
den Pfad ⎰   ⎱ the bank
                          the path

In German the *noun* (the thing you go up, down or along) comes *first*: in English it is at the end.

* * * * *

About "whose"

When asking a question, "Whose?" is always *Wessen?*

> Whose book is that? *Wessen* Buch ist das?
> With whose pen are you writing? Mit *wessen* Füllfeder schreiben Sie?

"Whose" can also be a form of the "who" and "which" dealt with in Lessons Nineteen and Twenty, in which case it will link up sentences with the verb at the end of its own part. In this sense the German word is *dessen* or *deren*. To understand why there are *two* words to choose between and to see how they work, look at the following examples:

> Der Arzt, *der* mit mir spricht, ist alt.
> Der *Arzt, dessen Frau* mit mir *spricht*, ist alt.
> Ich kenne ein *Mädchen, dessen Vater* in dem Metzgerladen *arbeitet.*
> Das Mädchen hat eine *Puppe, deren Haare* blond *sind.*
> Ich habe *Freunde, deren Haus* auf dem Land *steht.*

Whenever "whose" refers back to a der or das word, put *dessen.*

> (Der Arzt or das Mädchen, dessen . . . The doctor or the girl) whose . . .)

When it refers back to a die word or a plural, put *deren.*

> (Die Puppe or Freunde, deren . . . The doll or friends, whose . . .)

This is still true even if the first word has been affected, say, by a preposition. What matters is that it was *originally* der, das or die.

> Examples: Hinter *dem* Schüler, dessen . . .
> Von *der* Mutter, deren . . .

You will notice that the word *after* dessen or deren is always a *noun*. It can be of any type, singular or plural, but has *no* effect at all on the choice of dessen or deren, which is determined by the noun *in front*.

Word List 25

verbringen, to spend (time)	die Woche, the week
schwer, heavy	bei (List 2 prep.), with, at the house of

Exercise 25 (a)

Put into German:

1. Two men are sitting in a boat which is coming up the river.

2. Your neighbour's cat has run down the path in our garden.

3. A big car is going quickly along the road.

4. When I open the kitchen door, my dog runs out into the garden.

5. Whilst we are fishing near the bridge, the children are slowly climbing up the hill.

Join with the correct word for "whose":

6. Dieser alte Fahrgast sucht einen Gepäckträger. Sein Koffer ist sehr schwer.

7. Ich verbringe eine Woche bei meiner Tante. In ihrem Obstgarten darf ich Äpfel pflücken.

8. Der Organist spielt in einer Kirche. Der Turm dieser Kirche ist höher als die Häuser.

Complete:

9. Ich sehe einen Vogel, d—— Nest . . . .

10. Hans hat eine Schwester, d—— Taschentuch . . . . . .

Exercise 25 (b)

Put into English:

1. Mein Grossvater, dessen Pfeife auf den Teppich gefallen ist, ist in seinem bequemen Liegestuhl eingeschlafen.

2. Viele Kinder kommen den Waldweg entlanggelaufen.

3. Um seinen Ball zu suchen, klettert Erich auf das Dach der Garage hinauf.

4. Die Kinder spielen im Wald. Plötzlich springt Robert hinter einem grossen Baum hervor.

5. Ein Gärtner, dessen Schubkarre vor dem Fenster steht, hat heute unseren Garten umgegraben.

6. In wessen Pult haben Sie mein Lineal gesteckt?

Have a Try 25

Fit together three parts (one from each column) so as to make six correct sentences from the following. The verbs are given as infinitives: put them into the present tense.

Ein alter Brunnen	fallen	an der Endstation
Viele Fahrgäste	erzählen	in der Mittagspause
Eine lästige Fliege	schön aussehen	mitten auf dem Dorfplatz
Der junge Matrose	plätschern	im Juli
Unser Garten	sich gern ausruhen	in die Milch
Ein müder Gärtner	einsteigen	lustige Geschichten

HOW TO USE "DU". HOW TO SAY "HE WAS ARRESTED"

We mentioned *du* as long ago as Lesson Two. Although you must always use Sie for "you" when writing or speaking to adults and strangers, it is necessary to recognize du in letters and stories, and especially in the conversation of families and children.

We are now in a position to collect into one section everything that concerns du:

1. du ge*hst*, kauf*st*, schwimm*st*
du find*est*, öffn*est*

The verb-ending is -*st* except when impossible to pronounce, then -est.

du s*ie*hst, g*i*bst, schl*ä*fst

Verbs that change e to i(e) and a to ä with er, sie, es have the same change with du.

Learn separately du *wirst* ("you will"), du *musst* ("you must") du *bist* ("you are") and du *hast* ("you have"). The last two, remember, will be used very often with ge——.

2. ich kenne *dich*, ich sehe *dich*
ich sage *dir*, sitze neben *dir*

Dich and dir ("you" as object or after prepositions) can be compared with mich and mir.

3. *dein* Vater, *deine* Mutter
in *deinem* Schlafzimmer

Dein ("your") works exactly like mein and sein.

4. Commands:
Sprich! Gib! Nimm!
(Speak! Give! Take!)

These are the equivalent of Sprechen Sie! Geben Sie! etc. (Lesson Three). Only the "e" to "i" change takes place (not "a" to "ä") and there is *no* ending.

Schlaf(e)! Komme(e)! Such(e)!
Zeig(e)!
(Sleep! Come! etc.)

Other verbs often end in "e". The commoner ones tend to omit it, and you will often find Zeig'! Bring'! etc., with an apostrophe.

· · · · ·

Have you noticed how many *past participles* are used as adjectives ? Some of the commonest are:

überrascht (surprised)	zerbrochen (broken)
enttäuscht (disappointed)	umgeben (surrounded)

These frequently describe the *state* of a person or thing and are simply used with the verb "to be".

Ich bin enttäuscht. Gerdas Puppe ist zerbrochen.

(Notice that "frightened" is not done in this way. "I am frightened of cows" would be Ich *habe Angst* (lit. "have fear") *vor* Kühen, or ich fürchte mich.)

But "The dog *is punished*" or "The thief *is arrested*" are different. These are *actions*, not states: we really mean "The dog *gets* punished", "The thief *becomes* arrested".

This is exactly what we put in German, using *werden* in the special sense of "become" instead of the verb "to be":

Der Hund *wird* bestraft : Der Dieb *wird* verhaftet
(ich, of course, goes with werde and any plural with werden)

If we wish to add *"by"* someone, e.g. "by a policeman", this is a special use of *VON*: Der Dieb wird *von* einem Polizisten verhaftet.

Mind you don't get confused here. Werden + a past participle always means "is, becomes or gets ——ed", but werden + *infinitive* (Lesson Five) still means "will or shall ——", i.e. the future.

To finish this Lesson, let us learn in addition *"was"* and *"were"* punished, arrested, etc. This is something new; a past tense, but it is quite easy.

was punished, etc. = *WURDE* bestraft, etc.
were arrested, etc. = *WURDEN* verhaftet, etc.

This construction will be a great help to you later when you read a newspaper or a science book in German.

Word List 26

der Brunnen, the well
der Pass, the passport
das Fleisch, the meat

das Krankenhaus, the hospital
knurrig, growling
gestern, yesterday

Exercise 26 (*a*)

Rewrite in the du form:

1. Haben Sie ein Löschblatt in Ihrem Pult? 2. Geben Sie dem Lehrer Ihren Aufsatz! 3. Vergessen Sie nicht, dass Sie heute abend zum Friseur gehen müssen! 4. Darf ich Sie bitten, mir Ihren Pass zu zeigen? 5. Passen Sie auf! Hinter Ihnen steht ein knurriger Hund.

Put into English:

6. Ich möchte sehen, was du in der Tasche hast. 7. Lass mich mal sehen, wie du die Adresse schreibst! 8. Weil du der stärkste bist, sollst du den Koffer tragen. 9. Bist du noch da, Hans? Deine Freunde wollen mit dir sprechen. 10. Komm nur herein! Wir warten schon lange auf dich.

Exercise 26 (b)

Put into English:

1. In diesem kleinen Dorf wird Wasser aus einem alten Brunnen geholt. 2. Der Eimer wurde von der Putzfrau geleert. 3. Gestern wurde uns viel Geld angeboten. 4. Oft werden Geschichten von Matrosen erzählt. 5. Die Aufsätze dieser Kinder sind sehr schön geschrieben. 6. Letzte Woche wurde meine alte Grossmutter ins Krankenhaus gebracht.

Put into German:

7. This morning the roofs of the houses are covered with snow. 8. Meat is bought at the butcher's. (use bei)

(In the next four sentences use du, dich, dein, etc.)

9. Don't speak so loudly. Your brother has already gone to bed. 10. Why don't you want to eat your breakfast? 11. After you have dressed yourself, go downstairs. 12. Are you afraid of a little mouse?

Have a Try 26

From the Newspaper

Am Montagmorgen wurde Nordjapan von einem starken Erdbeben erschüttert. In der Nähe der Stadt Miyagi wurde eine Frau durch eine einstürzende Mauer erschlagen.

Am Dienstag wurde in Langenthal das neue Lehrerseminar eröffnet.

An der Sagenmattstrasse in Luzern sind Felsenmassen hinuntergestürzt und haben erheblichen Schaden angerichtet. Glücklicherweise wurde niemand verletzt. Ein Hund wurde lebend aus den Trümmern geborgen.

HOW TO SAY "I PLAYED" AND "I WAS PLAYING". "I *HAD* SEEN"

So far we have learnt three basic ways of using all our verbs. We can say, for instance

ich spiel*e* ("I play" or "am playing"—the present tense)
ich kann, werde, etc., spiel*en* (an "introductory" verb + infinitive)
ich habe *ge*spiel*t* (bin *ge*gang*en*)—("have" + past participle)

What we have not yet learnt is how to say "I *played*", that is, the simple *past tense*, without "have".

This is ich spiel*TE*.

Spielte also goes with er, sie and es: with *plurals* it adds -*N*, thus er spielte means "he played" and wir, Sie, sie or die Kinder spielten means "we, you, they or the children played".

This replacing of the English ending -ED by -TE(N) applies to all *weak* verbs. So we can say:

der Hund *bellte*, the dog barked   sie *holten*, they fetched
wir *tanzten*, we danced   ich *versuchte*, I tried

(du, by the way, needs -*test*: du spiel*test*, lern*test*, etc.)

Now for a most important discovery!

Spielte means not only "played", but also "*was playing*", "*used to play*" and "*did play*".

So this easy -TE(N) ending covers practically all the remaining "tense" forms we shall need. It will be most useful for *reading*, for most stories, as you will realize, make great use of it.

Here are some more examples:

Did he smoke? Rauchte er?   They used to live, sie wohnten
I wasn't dancing, ich tanzte nicht   We showed, wir zeigten

In this Lesson we can learn two more essential "past tenses":

120

WAR, "was" HATTE (singular), "had"
WAREN, "were" HATTEN (plural)
Der Arzt *war* im Sprechzimmer Wir *hatten* kein Geld

If we put these words with a *past participle*, they give us the last "tense" we require, i.e. "I *had* seen", "He *had* come", etc. Examples:

Ich hatte den Film schon gesehen
I had already seen the film

Das Auto war schnell um die Ecke gefahren
The car had gone quickly round the corner

Remember, the same verbs which needed ist instead of hat (Lesson Twenty-two) will have war instead of hatte.

.   .   .   .   .

Finally, one important detail. WENN is replaced by a new word, *ALS* (still with the verb *last*), when we refer to a non-repeated past action:

Wenn ich im Garten *arbeite*
but *Als* ich gestern im Garten *arbeitete*

Word List 27

das Handtuch, the towel
das Warenhaus, the big stores
anhören (W), to listen to
bestellen (W), to order

lachen (W), to laugh
hungrig, hungry
etwas, something
nichts, nothing

Exercise 27 (*a*)

Put into German:

1. The boy was putting something into his pocket when I opened the door. 2. The girl I danced with had brown hair. 3. My wife was knitting while she was listening to the wireless. 4. The light in my bedroom was not very bright. 5. A lot of tourists were buying tickets at the station. 6. After the joiner

had washed himself, he dried himself with a white towel. 7. We used to live in a bigger house. 8. Although we were so long in the big stores, we had bought nothing. 9. My brother laughed

when I showed him the picture. 10. Although I had fed my dog, he was still hungry.

Exercise 27 (b)

Put into English:

1. Während ich im Auto wartete, machte meine Schwester Einkäufe in der Stadt. 2. Ich war überrascht, als mein Wecker heute um halb sechs rasselte. 3. Das Kind verletzte sich, obgleich das Spielzeug nicht gefährlich war. 4. Im Sommer wanderten wir oft über die Hügel. 5. Der Kellner reichte mir ein Glas Wein, das ich im Café bestellt hatte. 6. Bald hatte mein Hund die schwarze Katze aus dem Garten gejagt. 7. Ich wartete im Krankenhaus, als ein Arzt plötzlich die Tür öffnete. 8. Als ich noch klein war, spielte ich oft mit der Puppe meiner Schwester. 9. Der Pfarrer schenkte seinem Sohn ein neues Fahrrad. 10. Das Mädchen hatte Angst vor dem grossen Pferd.

Exercise 27 (c)

Practise *aloud* all the verbs in the above exercises in the following forms:

ich mach*te*; wir mach*ten*; er *hatte ge*macht

Have a Try 27

Learn this piece of poetry by heart. (The harder words are given in the Key to help you get the meaning.)

Christmas
(Weihnachten)

Markt und Strassen stehn verlassen,
still erleuchtet jedes Haus;
sinnend geh' ich durch die Gassen,
alles sieht so festlich aus.

An den Fenstern haben Frauen
buntes Spielzeug fromm geschmückt,
tausend Kindlein stehn und schauen,
sind so wunderstill beglückt.

Und ich wandre aus den Mauern
bis hinaus ins freie Feld.
Hehres Glänzen, heil'ges Schauern—
wie so weit und still die Welt!

ABOUT "I SAW" AND "I WENT". HOW TO SAY "SOMETHING GOOD"

In the previous Lesson we were talking mainly about the past tense of "weak" verbs. Except for a few oddities such as "bought", their English equivalents end in *-ed*—"laugh*ed*" "work*ed*", order*ed*, etc.

But what happens to words such as "see", "write" or "find"? Instead of adding "-ed", these become "past" by changing their vowel: "s*ee*"—"s*aw*", "wr*i*te"—"wr*o*te", "f*i*nd"—"f*ou*nd".

A similar thing is done in German:

"saw" = s*a*h; "wrote" = schr*ie*b; "found" = f*a*nd (+EN in plural)

This is simply the *stem* with a new vowel; notice there is *no* ending with ich, er, sie or es, only -en with *plurals*.

To know what the new vowel is going to be, we need our Table from Lesson Twenty-four again: only in two cases is the change the same as in the past participle, but the same principle applies:

Infinitive	*Past Tense*
E	A
(l*e*sen)	(l*a*s)
(s*e*hen)	(s*a*h)
IE	O
(schl*ie*ssen)	(schl*o*ss)
I	A
(tr*i*nken)	(tr*a*nk)
(f*i*nden)	(f*a*nd)
A	IE or U
(f*a*llen)	(f*ie*l)
(f*a*hren)	(f*u*hr)
EI	IE
(schr*ei*ben)	(schr*ie*b)

A few verbs such as *"went"* and *"stood"* are made quite

irregularly from "go", "stand", etc. and must be learnt separately.

Here are the German equivalents:

"went", *ging*(en)   "caught", *fing*(en)
"came", *kam*(en)   "ran", *lief*(en)
"sat", *sass*(en)   "stood", *stand*(en)
              "brought", *brachte*(n)

(*N.B.* ziehen, *zog*(en))

We must also know the past tense of the kann type verbs in Lesson Five.

konnte(n), could, was (were) able to
wollte(n), wanted to
musste(n), had to
sollte(n), ought to, was (were) to
durfte(n), was (were) allowed to

Notice that none of these verbs has an umlaut. They will of course still be followed by an *infinitive*: the past of "I can go" is "I could *go*".

. . . . . .

There is something very interesting about the German way of saying

"something good" : "nothing new"

These are   etwas *Gutes* : nichts *Neues*

Any adjective with etwas or nichts has a *capital* and -*ES*.

Word List 28

der Engländer, the Englishman
die Feuerwehr, the fire-brigade
die Verkäuferin, the shop-girl
das Geschirr, the crockery
die Leute (pl), the people
ganz, whole

abräumen (W), to clear (tables)
aufbleiben, to stay up
emporsteigen, to rise up
Schlange stehen, to queue
skilaufen, to ski
ich gehe lieber, I prefer to go
würde(n) + infin., would (go, etc.)

Exercise 28 (*a*)

Join each pair of sentences with a conjunction or the word

for "who" or "which", and at the same time *change* the verbs
as indicated in brackets:

1. Karl steigt in den Autobus ein. Er will heute nachmittag
in die Stadt fahren. (GOT INTO . . . WANTED TO
GO . . .)

2. Hans fängt den Ball. Sein Freund wirft den Ball hoch in
die Luft. (CAUGHT . . . HAD THROWN . . .)

3. Gerda steht am Fenster. Ich komme ins Zimmer. (WAS
STANDING . . . CAME . . .)

4. Ich kann nicht sehr schnell laufen. Der Wind ist so stark.
(COULDN'T RUN . . . WAS . . .)

5. Die Maus hat Angst vor der Katze. Die Maus kriecht
in ihr Loch. (WAS AFRAID . . . HAD CREPT . . .)

Put into German:

6. The professor was reading a magazine which he had
bought at the station.

7. Hans still wanted to ski, although he had hurt himself on
Monday.

8. When I had shut the door, the policeman tried to open it again.

9. Why did Robert go to bed before he had drunk his milk?

10. We had to wait a long time before (say "bis"—"until") the doctor came.

Exercise 28 (b)

Put into English:

1. Wir fuhren lieber mit der Untergrundbahn, weil soviele Leute an der Haltestelle Schlange standen.

2. Nachdem wir den Tisch abgeräumt hatten, wurde das Geschirr in die Küche getragen.

3. Als die Feuerwehr ankam, stieg schwarzer Rauch vom Dach des Rathauses empor.

4. Ein Engländer fragte die Verkäuferin, ob sie ihm eine billige Uhr zeigen würde.

5. Ich habe im ganzen Laden nichts Besseres gefunden.

6. Hans kam schnell in das Dorf herunter, weil er gut skilaufen konnte.

7. Um halb sieben war das kleine Kind schon eingeschlafen.

Complete:

8. Weil ich ei— neu— Hemd kauf— w——te, m—— ich —— Laden geh—.

9. Der Junge h—— Angst, weil er hinter d— Kirche et—— Weiss— ge—— h—te.

10. Hans dur—— bis halb elf aufbl——, weil sei— Onkel uns besuch—.

Have a Try 28

Franz Ahlmeyer hatte den Abend bei einigen Freunden verbracht und kehrte nun sehr spät nach Hause zurück. Als er die Schlossstrasse entlang wanderte, sah er plötzlich einen Mann auf dem Pflaster liegen. Er beugte sich überrascht über ihn und versuchte, ihn zu wecken. Dann sah er aber, dass er

Blut an den Fingern hatte. Es war klar, dass der arme Mensch tot war.

Während er noch überlegte, was er da machen sollte, kamen zwei Polizisten herbei. Sobald sie den Toten erblickten, nahmen sie Franz gefangen und brachten ihn auf die Polizeiwache, wo er gründlich ausgefragt wurde. Er sagte: „Ich weiss gar nichts von der Sache", aber man wollte ihm nicht glauben.

Zum Entsetzen seiner Familie wurde er sofort ins Gefängnis geworfen, obgleich er wusste, dass er unschuldig war.

HOW TO MAKE NEW NOUNS. MORE CONVERSATION

You will have realized by this stage that a very important feature of German is the making of new words by joining together two or more shorter ones. Just consider Bahnsteig, Hausflur or Fahrgast.

If you continue to study German, more and more of the new words you need will prove to be compounds of words you already know. An attic, for example, is simply ein Dachzimmer ("roof-room"). Even "hydrogen", which sounds quite difficult, is only Wasserstoff ("water-stuff")!

It will be useful if we collect together in this Lesson the main methods of making nouns of this kind.

1. Noun + noun.

> e.g. Briefpapier, writing-paper   Regenbogen, rainbow

Sometimes an "s" comes in between (Schiffsarzt : ship's doctor) or if the first word ends in -e, it loses the "e" or adds "n" (Schulzimmer, Sonnenschein).

2. Stem of verb + noun.

> e.g. *Fahr*karte, *Sprech*zimmer (consulting room)

3. Adjective + noun.

> e.g. *Klein*geld (change); *Schnell*zug (express train)

4. Sometimes an "ending" is added: e.g. Freund*schaft* (friend*ship*). (All words ending in -schaft are die words.)

There are also nouns which are developed from verbs. Die Schrift, for instance, is connected with schreiben:

> die Inschrift, inscription; die Vorschrift, prescription

Der Gang is the noun from gehen. You will often see Ausgang (exit).

. . . . .

In conversation, short remarks such as "Of course!" are really more useful than long sentences. Here are a few in German for you to learn:

Jawohl! Oh yes! Wirklich? Really? Also gut, Very well. Gewiss! Certainly! Wieso denn? How do you mean? Leider nicht, Unfortunately not. Natürlich! Of course! Durchaus nicht, Not at all. Auf Wiedersehen! Good bye! Guten Tag! Good day! Entschuldigen Sie! (or Verzeihen Sie!), Excuse me! Ich bin Ihnen sehr dankbar, I'm very grateful to you. Bitte sehr! Don't mention it! Es freut mich sehr, I'm delighted. Doch! Oh yes I do! (after a negative) e.g. Sie schwimmen nicht? Doch! Hoffentlich, I hope

Word List 29

der Eintritt, entry, admission	ähnlich, similar
der Platz, the seat	amüsieren (sich) (W), to have a good time
der Schirm, "protective cover"	
die Bürste, the brush	besorgen (W), to see to, get
die Nähe, the vicinity	ein bisschen, a little, a bit
die Kasse, the cash-desk	gerade, just
die Reihe, the row	hin und zurück, there and back (return)
die Zigarre, the cigar	
das Halstuch, the scarf	teuer, dear, expensive
	versprechen, to promise

Exercise 29 (a)

Give the English for:

die Schreibmaschine, die Hängebrücke, die Rauchwolke, der Bergsteiger, die Brieftasche, der Zeigefinger, die Grossstadt, der Schlafwagen, die Zahnbürste, der Fallschirm, das Puppenspiel, der Fussgänger, die Nachbarschaft, die Schallplatte (lit. "sound-plate"), das Treibrad.

What are the following in German?

an apple-tree, a pitcher (for water), a hair-brush, dance

music, a sea-voyage, writing paper, a bread-knife, a girls' school, "way in", an umbrella, a class-room, the garden wall.

Exercise 29 (b)

Put into English:

1. Kennen Sie vielleicht einen guten Arzt in der Nähe? Gewiss. Der berühmte Doktor Cranach wohnt gerade um die Ecke im ersten Gebäude. 2. Dieses Halstuch ist mir ein bisschen zu teuer. Haben Sie etwas Ähnliches zu drei Mark? Leider nicht. 3. Haben Sie einige Aufnahmen gemacht, als wir Schloss Thorstein besuchten? Aber natürlich! Wir

versprechen uns viel davon. 4. Heute abend wollen wir ins Theater gehen. Hoffentlich haben Sie nicht vergessen, die Eintrittskarten zu besorgen? 5. Darf ich Ihnen eine Zigarre anbieten, oder rauchen Sie vielleicht nicht? Doch! Ich rauche sehr gern.

Put into German:

6. I would like two seats for this evening. How much are these here in the second row? 7. I am delighted that you have had such a good time. 8. Can you please change this 50-Mark note for me? Certainly: please come to the cash-desk. 9. You can't get into the train, because you have only a platform-ticket. 10. What is the fare (how much is it) to Heidelberg, please? Five marks? Very well, two second class tickets (Fahrkarten zweiter Klasse), return, please.

Have a Try 29

Der Tag der Abreise war da. Schon am vorigen Abend hatten wir uns lange mit dem Einpacken beschäftigt, denn wir mussten sehr früh aufstehen. Nach dem Frühstück begleiteten uns unsere Freunde zum Bahnhof und sorgten dafür, dass wir den richtigen Zug und gute Plätze bekamen.

Mit unserem Aufenthalt in Deutschland waren wir sehr zufrieden. Während der letzten vierzehn Tage hatten wir allerlei Ausflüge gemacht, und überall waren die Leute nett und freundlich gewesen. In der deutschen Sprache waren wir auch schon ziemlich bewandert. Das waren wirklich die glücklichsten Ferien, dir wir je verlebt hatten!

HOW TO SAY "INSTEAD OF". A LAST
LOOK ROUND

Our last Lesson includes most of the remaining expressions and types of sentence you will find in everyday German. If it seems rather long, perhaps it would be best to have two "bites" at it!

First come three more prepositions: während (during), anstatt (instead of) and mittels (by means of).

This is how they are used:

> während *des* Sommers, during the summer
> anstatt *einer* Zeitung, instead of a newspaper
> mittels *eines* Hammers, by means of a hammer

Unlike any of the prepositions in our Lists 1 and 2, these are followed by the "of" endings of Lesson Ten, and therefore form a separate group of their own. (There are a few more words of this kind, but these three are good representatives.)

Next we will look at a number of expressions using machen (literally "make") where in English we use a different verb.

> ich *mache* einen Spaziergang — I *go for* a walk (a trip)
>   (einen Ausflug)
> ich *mache* Einkäufe   — I *do* (some) shopping
> ich *mache* Aufnahmen   — I *take* photographs
> es *macht* mir Vergnügen — it *gives* me pleasure

The rest of the points are a "mixed bag" that we will divide up into sections.

(*a*) We ought to know how to say "Let's go!" "Let's buy it!", etc.

This is simply *Gehen wir! Kaufen wir* es! and so on.

(*b*) "There is" and "There are" start off lots of sentences. In German, *both* of these are *Es gibt* (when the *place* is not mentioned):

Es gibt nichts Neues, There is nothing new
Es gibt Fische, die fliegen können, There are fish that can fly

("There was" and "There were" would both be Es *gab*.)
When the place *is* mentioned, you must put Es *ist* and Es
sind:

Es ist Butter im Kühlschrank, There is butter in the refrigerator
Es sind Blumen im Garten, There are flowers in the garden

(This time, "There was (were)" would be Es war (waren).)

(*c*) The word "*some*" is often misunderstood.
When it means "a quantity of *one* thing" it is *etwas*:

etwas Papier, some paper   etwas Wasser, some water

With *plurals*, meaning "a few", it is *einige*:

einige Bücher, some (a few) books   einige Vögel, some birds

(*d*) "*Outside*" is another confusing word, especially if you
are relying on a small dictionary.

Ich stehe (warte, sitze) *draussen* (used when there is no noun to
say "outside *what*" and no *movement*).
Ich gehe aus (or hinaus) (no noun, but movement, meaning "*to*
outside").
Ich warte *vor* der Kirche, "I'll wait outside the church" (when
the place is mentioned).

(*e*) You will be sure to see and hear two words *hätte(n)* and
wäre(n) followed by adjectives or past participles, thus:

Es *wäre schön*; ich *hätte gespielt*; wir *wären gegangen*

These mean "it *would be* nice"; "I *would have* played"; "we
would have gone".
Used in this way, hätte and wäre (+ n in plural) are "short
cuts" for "would have" and "would be".

(*f*) The little word *kaum*, meaning "scarcely" or "hardly",
produces an interesting kind of sentence:

Kaum hatte der Arzt gesprochen, *als* die Tür sich *öffnete*
Hardly had the doctor spoken, when the door opened

(g) Finally there is the peculiar construction "the bigger, the better", "the quicker, the sooner", etc.

This is *je* grösser, *desto* besser; *je* schneller, *desto* früher, etc. In a complete sentence, the pattern is as follows:

Je schneller ich *laufe*, desto früher *erreiche* ich den Bahnhof
(Je ——er . . . (verb *last*), desto ——er (verb *next*) . . .)

Word List 30

der Helm, the helmet	glauben (W), to believe
befehlen, to order	sammeln (W), to collect
(*N.B.* ich befehle ih*m*)	schicken (W), to send
erreichen (W), to reach (places)	kurz, short

Exercise 30 (a)

Put into English:

1. Laufen wir den Hügel hinunter! Es sind uns keine Bäume im Weg. 2. Während des Winters können wir oft über die Felder skilaufen. 3. Je höher wir steigen, desto kälter wird die Luft. 4. Vor der Mädchenschule macht eine alte Lehrerin einen kurzen Spaziergang. 5. Ein Wörterbuch wäre nützlich, wenn Sie mir etwas schenken wollten. 6. Kaum hatten wir die Einkäufe gemacht, als schwarze Wolken begannen, sich am

Himmel zu sammeln. 7. Es hat uns viel Vergnügen gemacht, den Abend bei Ihnen zu verbringen. 8. Anstatt einer Mütze trägt dieser Polizist einen Helm. 9. Einige Touristen, die gestern angekommen sind, machen heute morgen einen Ausflug ins nächste Dorf. 10. Das hätte ich nie geglaubt.

Exercise 30 (b)

Put into German:

1. There are people who have never played cricket. 2. There were some apples under the trees in the orchard. 3. I would like to send some flowers to my grandmother. 4. Please wait outside. There are too many people in the room already. 5. The more comfortable my bed is, the longer I sleep. 6. Hardly had the passengers got into the bus, when the

conductor ordered them to get out again. 7. It's very cold outside. Let's give the birds some bread. 8. Hardly had we reached the hotel, when our friends arrived. 9. That girl is looking at us; let's take a photo! 10. During the evening I have written two letters.

Exercise 30 (c)

Write in German a short paragraph on each of the following subjects:

(a) In der Stadt.   (b) Meine Freunde.

Use this exercise to practise as many different kinds of sentence as possible, including some conversation.

Have a Try 30

To finish with, here is an interesting puzzle. Now that you have done all the Lessons, take your time over it!

Arrange the syllables below to form twenty-three words answering the clues given. Write these words in order opposite the clues, and you will find their *first* and *last* letters, read downwards, make up a "saying":

Syllables

a au ca car che de de di di e ei en eu
eu ex ex fen freg ger ger gi graph ha hop i
in ju la land le le ler li lo men mi na ne
nur ohr on pen po ra rem rew ri ri ser sin
star stri te tes ti tief to trakt um val wei

Clues

1. Tiroler Maler.
2. Kirchensonntag.
3. Grundstoff.
4. Orientalisches Frauengemach.
5. Phönizische Göttin.
6. Mathematiker.
7. Italienischer Opernkomponist.
8. Oper von d'Albert.
9. Schlangenlinie.
10. Berg im Berner Oberland.
11. Halbinsel der Adria.
12. Finnischer Sportsmann.
13. Umstellschiene.
14. Nachtvogel.
15. Bergmassiv am Vierwaldstätter See.
16. Kanton der Schweiz.
17. Nebenfluss des Bug.
18. Beleidigung.
19. Oper von Bizet.
20. Bestandteil des Biers.
21. Kartenzeichner.
22. Operngestalt von Saint-Saëns.
23. Starker Drogenauszug.

PART II

KEY TO EXERCISES

Exercise 1 (*a*)

1. The mother fetches the bread. 2. The grandfather has spectacles and a newspaper. 3. The girl has a doll. The doll is pretty. 4. This ball is round. 5. This house is small, but the street is wide. 6. The family lives here. 7. That shop is open. 8. Who is Charles? Charles is the son. Charles is a boy. 9. What is the dog like? The dog is white. 10. Every son is a boy. 11. The grandfather has a pipe.

Exercise 1 (*b*)

1. Dieses Zimmer ist hell. 2. Jener Hund sucht Karl. 3. Dieser Laden ist klein. 4. Die Mutter ruft das Mädchen. 5. Ein Junge spielt hier. 6. Jener Hund holt eine Zeitung. 7. Der Hund bellt laut. 8. Wie ist dieses Brot? 9. Wo ist jener Ball? 10. Ein Zimmer hat eine Tür. 11. Ist jedes Mädchen hübsch? 12. Wer wohnt hier?

Have a Try 1

Helga brings her doll into the room. The grandfather is looking (looks) everywhere for his spectacles. Without spectacles (glasses) he can't read the newspaper. He is smoking a pipe. Here lies the dog, and there is a ball. The boy often plays with the ball in the garden. What is the mother doing? She fetches the bread, and the family comes into the dining-room. The dinner smells good, and they all eat heartily!

Exercise 2 (*a*)

Any verb in the list will do, provided that it ends in -*t* and makes good sense. Some possible answers are:

> der Freund radelt; steht nicht
> ein Mädchen tanzt; hämmert nicht
> die Tante schreibt; schwimmt nicht
> ein Vogel fliegt; beisst nicht

Exercise 2 (*b*)

1. Where is the station, please? 2. Do you play the piano? 3. This boy hasn't a toy. 4. Do the uncle and the aunt live next door? 5. Does a dog fly? No, it (he) doesn't fly. 6. Nein, er strickt nicht (er hämmert, angelt, etc.) 7. Das Hotel (or es) ist klein (gross, offen). 8. Ja, ich habe ein Auto (or Nein, ich habe kein Auto). 9. Ist eine Apfelsine blau (grün)? 10. Strickt die Grossmutter? 11. Wer steht dort? (or Wo steht der Onkel?) 12. Wie ist der Himmel? (or *der* Ball, *der* Vogel).

Exercise 2 (*c*)

1. Beisst dieser Hund? Nein, er beisst nicht. 2. Tragen Sie eine Jacke? 3. Dieser Garten ist nicht sehr gross. 4. Tanzt jenes Mädchen? 5. Suchen Sie die Post? 6. Dieser Apfel ist nicht grün. 7. Wo ist das Hotel? 8. Ist jener Vogel gelb? 9. Nein, wir singen nicht. 10. Spielt ein Junge nebenan (das) Klavier?

Have a Try 2

A car is standing outside the post-office and our neighbour gets out. Why does he go into the post-office? He has no stamps and must (has to) post a letter. A boy comes into the street where my uncle lives and goes to the door of his house. The dog doesn't bark, for he knows Charles. My aunt gives him an orange. Next door a man is working in the garden, for the sky is blue and it isn't raining.

Exercise 3 (*a*)

ich halt*e* mein*en* Schlüssel
Karl *nimmt* sein*en* Kugelschreiber
Grete such*t* ihr*en* Farbstift
wir pfleg*en* uns*eren* Garten
Sie find*en* I*hr* Lineal
sie sieh*t* (or sie seh*en*) ihr*en* Bruder
dieser Junge *trifft* sein*e* Schwester

Exercise 3 (*b*)

1. Holen Sie Ihr Glas! 2. Hat der Gärtner seine Schubkarre? 3. Die Putzfrau leert ihren Eimer. 4. Zerbrechen Sie nicht jenen Krug! 5. Haben Sie mein Lineal? 6. Inge nimmt ihre Feder und schreibe inen Brief. 7. Geben Sie mir Ihr Taschenmesser! 8. Meine Schwester trägt ihre Puppe nicht. 9. Hat Ihr Vater seinen Schlüssel? 10. Der Kellner bringt mir einen Teller. 11. Es ist kalt; der Tau fällt. 12. Zeigen Sie mir Ihre Jacke!

Exercise 3 (*c*)

1. Nimmt dieser Junge sein Taschenmesser? 2. Mein Vater liest seinen Brief. 3. Wirft Ihr Bruder seinen Ball? 4. Leeren Sie dieses Trinkglas! 5. Unsere Putzfrau hat ihren Eimer.

6. Don't break my ball-point pen. 7. Does the gardener chase (Is the gardener chasing) that dog? 8. Fetch an apple and a plate. 9. Hans (Jack) throws his ball over the wall. 10. Have you a brother or a sister?

Have a Try 3

A gardener is working in the park. He is digging over the

flowerbeds and pushes his wheelbarrow along the path. The roses are blooming in the bright sunshine. A bird perches on the wheelbarrow, for it sees a fat worm. The gardener has to water the flowers in the evening, if it doesn't rain. The grass is short, for he has a good lawn-mower.

Exercise 4 (a)

In the kitchen	*In the bedroom*	*In the living-room*
der praktische Kühlschrank	dieser weiche Teppich	unser neues Radio
eine elektrische Küchenuhr	mein bequemer Stuhl	das lange Büfett
der tiefe Spülstein	ein zuverlässiger Wecker	jenes schöne Bild
ein grosses Feuer	der hohe Kleiderschrank	eine bunte Blumenvase

(Some of these could be varied: der Teppich could be in the living-room, neu could go with Kühlschrank, for example.)

Exercise 4 (b)

1. Has your neighbour a new car? 2. Oh dear, we haven't any fresh bread. 3. Is that little shop open? I would like a juicy orange. 4. Charles' new alarm-clock is ringing; he is having a long sleep this morning. 5. This pretty girl shows me her little doll. 6. What have you in your pocket, Jack? I have my sharp penknife, a rusty key, this dirty handkerchief and a broken watch. 7. Bring me a clean tumbler. 8. Charles breaks that big jug. 9. A little dachshund fetches my new ball. 10. My old grandmother isn't reading; she is knitting a green pullover.

Exercise 4 (c)

1. Mein kleiner Bruder schwimmt nicht. 2. Hämmern Sie nicht so laut! 3. Wo arbeitet der alte Gärtner? 4. Dieser weisse Hund läuft nicht. 5. Die Putzfrau trägt einen leeren Eimer.

6. Mein altes Lineal ist kaputt, aber ich habe einen neuen Kugelschreiber. 7. Gehen Sie nicht! Hier ist ein sehr

bequemer Stuhl. 8. Ich möchte lesen, aber mein Nachbar zeigt uns sein neues Auto. 9. Wo ist (steht) der neue Kühlschrank? 10. Sehen Sie jenen gelben Vogel?

Have a Try 4

Rendsheim is a little village in Germany. Next week we are spending our holidays there. A clear stream flows through the pretty (nice) village, and we fish and swim in the cool water. I go into a big (wide) field, where an old man is working. I pick a red apple in the orchard. (The) summer is really the most beautiful time of year (season).

Exercise 5 (a)

1. Dieses Mädchen kann gut tanzen. 2. Ich muss ein gutes Hotel suchen. 3. Wollen Sie einen roten Farbstift kaufen? 4. Der Zug wird den Bahnhof verlassen. 5. Wir möchten das Radio hören.

6. We are not to smoke. 7. A dog can't fly. 8. Will your sister bring the green vase? 9. May we go into the village this morning? 10. My grandfather likes to read (reading) the newspaper.

Exercise 5 (b)

1. Möchten Sie meinen Bruder treffen? 2. Ein Tischler kann einen Tisch machen. 3. Sie dürfen etwas Wasser in mein Trinkglas giessen. 4. Ich werde mein Hotel suchen. 5. Wir müssen durch diesen dichten Wald gehen. 6. Mein kleiner Hund will draussen spielen; er geht an die Tür. 7. Können Sie das Brot holen? 8. Jedes Mädchen möchte eine schöne Puppe haben. 9. Ich kann nicht ohne (eine) Feder schreiben. 10. Unser Nachbar angelt gern. 11. Das Brot fällt auf den Teppich. 12. Jener Vogel fliegt gegen den Wind.

Have a Try 5

My German pen-friend wants to (or "is going to") visit us in London next year. He has been learning English for three years and often sends me a very interesting letter from Hamburg. He is very keen on ships and steamers. He likes rowing, too. We are sure to spend a lot of time by the Thames (lit. "shall surely spend").

Exercise 6 (a)

1. Ist Herr Schneider zu Hause? 2. Frau Schmidt muss in der Küche arbeiten. 3. Karl kommt mit seinem kleinen Bruder aus jenem grünen Wald. 4. Eine Blumenvase steht in diesem Zimmer auf dem Tisch, nicht wahr? 5. Fräulein Kleber sitzt am Fenster. 6. Ich wandere nicht gern durch den tiefen Schnee.

Exercise 6 (b)

1. Ich muss mit meinem neuen Kugelschreiber einen Brief schreiben. 2. Frau Meyer schneidet das Brot mit einem scharfen Messer. 3. Können Sie einen Schlüssel auf meinem Pult sehen? 4. Mein kleiner Hund läuft aus dem Zimmer. 5. Herr Kleber schläft in einem bequemen Bett. 6. Ich muss morgen zum Arzt gehen. 7. Sie möchten (gern) auf dem Land wohnen, nicht wahr? 8. Ich soll nach dem Frühstück im Garten arbeiten. 9. Herr Meyer vom Hotel will mit Ihrem Bruder sprechen. 10. Mein Wecker steht auf einem kleinen Tisch in meinem Schlafzimmer.

Exercise 6 (c)

Several combinations are possible. The following are the best:

> Der Gärtner kommt in den Garten (steht in dem (im) Garten).
> Mein Lineal liegt auf dem Tisch (mit dem Löschblatt).

Ein Vorhang hängt an dem (einem) Fenster.
Die Milch steht in dem (unserem, etc.) Kühlschrank.
Ein Bild hängt an der (dieser, etc.) Wand.
Das Trinkglas steht auf dem Tisch (im Kühlschrank).
Das Brot liegt auf einem Teller (dem Tisch).
Unser Auto kommt aus der Garage (steht in der Garage).
Ein Zug kommt in den Bahnhof (steht im Bahnhof, kommt aus dem Bahnhof).
Die Sonne steht am Himmel.

Have a Try 6

1. Baum 2. Blatt 3. Brücke 4. Tinte 5. Marktplatz
6. Freund 7. Fliege 8. Tischtuch.

Exercise 7 (a)

1. Mit seinem Modellflugzeug spielt mein kleiner Bruder im Garten. 2. Mit der Schere schneidet meine Mutter die Wolle. 3. In der Kirche spielt der Organist die Orgel. 4. Nach dem Frühstück muss ich in das Büro gehen. 5. Auf dem Gasherd kochen wir das Mittagessen.

6. Am Morgen springe ich gern aus dem Bett. 7. Am Abend sitzen wir zu Hause und sehen (uns) das Fernsehprogramm an. 8. Jetzt schreibe ich diese Aufgabe. 9. Langsam muss ein Zug in den Bahnhof einfahren. 10. Draussen kann ich im Wald wandern.

Exercise 7 (b)

1. Auf dem Dach kann ich einen Vogel sehen. 2. Lesen Sie mir Ihren Brief vor! 3. Natürlich schlafe ich nach meinem Abendessen ein. 4. Unten macht jemand das Frühstück. 5. Jetzt muss ich aufstehen.

1. Überall liegt Schnee. 2. Leise spricht das Mädchen mit ihrer Grossmutter. 3. Oft muss ich Brot im Laden holen.

4. In der Küche darf mein Hund schlafen. 5. Bald wird die Sonne aufgehen.

Have a Try 7

In Berlin people like travelling by Tube. Often you have to stand and "strap-hang". But it's not so quick by bus. People get in and out (on and off) at every stop.

In an Underground carriage you can read a book, if the journey is (lasts) fairly long. Of course you can't spread a newspaper out in a crowded (full) carriage!

Exercise 8 (*a*)

diese Schlüssel; unsere (or meine) Taschen; die Stühle; die Länder; Aufgaben; jene Bilder; die Pferde; diese Kirchtürme; welche Züge; die Schlösser.

Exercise 8 (*b*)

der ——e Berg	ein ——er Berg	——e Berge
das ——e Licht	ein ——es Licht	——e Lichter
der ——e Fluss	ein ——er Fluss	——e Flüsse
die ——e Brücke	eine ——e Brücke	——e Brücken
die ——e Wolke	eine ——e Wolke	——e Wolken
der ——e Teller	ein ——er Teller	——e Teller
das ——e Haus	ein ——es Haus	——e Häuser
der ——e Tennisball	ein ——er Tennisball	——e Tennisbälle
das ——e Trinkglas	ein ——es Trinkglas	——e Trinkgläser
die ——e Banane	eine ——e Banane	——e Bananen

Exercise 8 (*c*)

1. On the walls beautiful pictures are hanging. 2. The white clouds drift (sail) across the green fields. 3. My brothers have pencils, knives and handkerchiefs in their (lit. "the") pockets.

4. Hinter diesen kleinen Dörfern sehen wir grosse Berge. 5. In den blauen Vasen sehe ich bunte Blumen. 6. Grosse Bäume wachsen in jenen schönen Wäldern.

7. Apfelsinen liegen auf unseren Tellern. 8. Schöne Autos stehen in unseren Garagen. 9. Wir können reife Äpfel an jenen Bäumen sehen. 10. Jene Kinder singen schöne Lieder.

Have a Try 8

The Rhine is a famous German river. A lot of people have trips on the Rhine steamers. On the banks they see castles. With a camera you (they) can take all kinds of photos. Later they show them to their friends. Villages, towns and vineyards are situated not far from the river. You can also go for long walks through cool woods.

Exercise 9 (a)

1. Für uns. 2. Ich möchte Sie treffen. 3. Holen Sie sie! 4. Können Sie mich hören? 5. Ohne sie. 6. Mit mir. 7. Fragen Sie sie! 8. Ich sitze neben Ihnen. 9. Daraus. 10. Für mich.

Exercise 9 (b)

1. Ich muss eine Briefmarke auf diesen Brief kleben. 2. Der Vater hält seine Pfeife zwischen den Zähnen. 3. Ich setze meine Mütze auf den Kopf. 4. Der Hund läuft über den Teppich und kriecht unter einen Stuhl. 5. Ein Taxi hält vor dem Bahnhof.

Exercise 9 (c)

1. Hinter diesen hohen Zäunen liegen schöne Gärten. 2. In den Schaufenstern sehen wir bunte Badeanzüge. 3. Weisse

Wolken ziehen über die grünen Felder. 4. An den Wänden hängen schöne Bilder. 5. Unsere kleinen Brüder wollen neue Spielzeuge kaufen.

1. Giessen Sie die Milch in ein Glas! 2. Stecken Sie dieses Geld in die Tasche! 3. Wörterbücher sind nützlich; wir suchen Wörter darin. 4. Hunde sind Haustiere. 5. Sehen Sie jenen Tisch? Darauf sind blaue Blumen.

Have a Try 9

In hot weather we all go to the swimming-bath. Boys and girls in gay swimming-costumes are swimming or splashing about in the clear water. The bigger boys are diving boldly from the springboard, but the smaller children are afraid of getting out of their depth.

After half an hour we are often tired. Then we like to sit at the edge of the bath and watch the better ("more efficient") swimmers.

Exercise 10 (a)

    die Schubkarre des alten Gärtners
    der Kugelschreiber meines kleinen Bruders
    die Tür jenes grossen Kleiderschranks
    die Orgel dieser schönen Kirche
    das Wasser eines tiefen Flusses
    die Schere meiner alten Grossmutter
    die Zweige der grünen Bäume
    der Hut jenes hübschen Mädchens
    die Farbstifte der kleinen Kinder
    die Räder unseres neuen Autos

Exercise 10 (b)

1. In dem Schaufenster dieses modernen Ladens kann ich einen elektrischen Kühlschrank sehen.

2. Die Schwester jenes berühmten Arztes steckt rote Rosen in eine bunte Blumenvase.

3. Nach einem langen Spaziergang durch die herbstlichen Wälder muss ich meine nassen Schuhe sofort ausziehen.

4. Hungrige Leute sitzen an den bequemen Tischen im Speisezimmer dieses neuen Hotels.

5. Über die hohe Mauer des langen Gartens klettert ein schmutziger Junge und sucht seinen Ball unter den Blumen.

Exercise 10 (c)

1. Der Briefträger öffnet mit einem grossen Schlüssel den Briefkasten.

2. Unser kleiner Hund liegt gern auf dem Bett meines Bruders.

3. Oft kaufe ich ein Speiseeis im kleinen Café an der Ecke unserer Strasse.

4. Möchten Sie ein Glas Milch (trinken)? 5. Finden Sie das Wörterbuch Ihrer Schwester nützlich? 6. Nie esse ich (Ich esse nie) die Schale eines Apfels. 7. Die weissen Wolken ziehen über die Gipfel der hohen Berge. 8. Holen Sie die scharfe Schere aus meinem Nähkasten! 9. Vor den grossen Fenstern meines Schlafzimmers hängen weisse Vorhänge. 10. Ein schöner Baum mit grünen Blättern wächst im Garten des Arztes.

Have a Try 10

A party of children are having a hike in the country. The path leads through woods and villages, but at last they see near a lovely river the brightly lit windows of a modern building.

This is the youth hostel. You write your name in a big book and show your membership card. Then you can sit down at the long table and look forward to a good supper. In another room you can play chess or cards.

Exercise 11 (a)

siebzehn, siebenundzwanzig, siebenmal drei ist einundzwanzig, fünfzehn weniger vier ist elf, drei und neun ist zwölf, dreissig durch zwei ist fünfzehn, neunzehn weniger fünf ist vierzehn, sechs und zehn ist sechzehn, vierundzwanzig durch drei ist acht, sechsmal fünf ist dreissig.

Exercise 11 (b)

vier Räder, zwanzig Pfund, zehn Mark, drei Jahre, sechs Fuss, acht Kilometer, fünf Hunde, zwei Bilder, drei Männer, dreissig Grad.

Exercise 11 (c)

1. The grandmother gives the little girl a new watch (as a present).
2. Jack tells his mother the truth. 3. Please give me my fountain pen.
4. The dachshund often brings my grandfather the paper.
5. The doctor offers a chair to my aunt.

6. Der Matrose erzählt den Kindern eine lange Geschichte. 7. Der Kellner bringt meinem Freund ein Glas. 8. Unser Nachbar bietet meiner Mutter (einige) Blumen an. 9. Der Junge zeigt seiner Schwester das Nest des Vogels. 10. Zuweilen muss ich meiner Mutter ihre Brille reichen.

Have a Try 11

It is a nice summer day. The sun shines down from a cloudless sky. Already a large crowd is thronging the riverside, for a lot of crews are rowing on the river today. Two boats are standing (waiting) at the landing-stage, a third is already moving. Out of the boat-house come some young men in shorts, each with a white pullover. Now they are grasping the oars. Soon the contest will begin (lit. "begins").

Exercise 12 (*a*)

Ich gehe zum Friseur, weil (wenn) meine Haare zu lang sind.

Ich stehe schnell auf, wenn mein Wecker am Morgen rasselt.

Wir müssen auf dem Bahnsteig warten, bis der Zug in den Bahnhof kommt.

Meine Grossmutter strickt einen Pullover, während mein Vater die Zeitung liest.

Ich muss um zehn Uhr zu Bett gehen, obgleich ich nicht schläfrig bin.

Exercise 12 (*b*)

1. I must go to the sports-shop when I want to buy a new tennis racket. 2. We are not allowed to get into a compartment whilst the train is still moving. 3. I often play the piano because I think music is so delightful. 4. The organist plays quietly until the service begins. 5. The butter is still fresh, although we have no refrigerator.

6. Mein Grossvater ist fünfundsiebzig Jahre alt. 7. Dieser Fernsehapparat kostet achthundertsechsundvierzig Mark. 8. Ich gehe sofort zu Bett, wenn ich vom Theater nach Hause komme. 9. Dieser Hund ist so dick, dass er nicht laufen kann. 10. Hans muss seine Schulaufgaben machen, ehe er Kricket spielt.

Have a Try 12

Some possible answers:

2. Ich kann lesen, wenn ich ein interessantes Buch habe.

3. Wir wollen in den Wald gehen, obgleich die Sonne nicht scheint.

4. Zwei Hunde haben acht Beine, weil ein Hund vier Beine hat.

5. Wir sitzen immer im Garten, bis meine Frau uns ruft.

Exercise 13 (*a*)

1. Can you please tell me how to get to the town-hall? 2. Go straight on, then round the corner to the left, and you'll come straight to the town-hall. 3. My wife often asks me to do some shopping in (the) town. 4. I must ask a porter from which platform the 9 o'clock train leaves. 5. The charlady puts her bucket in(to) the corner of the room. 6. In the market you can buy all kinds of vegetables. 7. My wife is asking a fat man to shut the carriage window.

8. Legen Sie Ihre Jacke auf das Bett! 9. Wie heisst der Junge nebenan? 10. Ich stelle meine Schuhe unter einen Stuhl, wenn ich zu Bett gehe. 11. Wieviel kostet jener Kricketschläger im Schaufenster? 12. Können Sie mir bitte sagen, wo ich eine Zeitung kaufen kann? 13. Stecken Sie frische Blumen in jene Vase! 14. Bitten Sie meinen Bruder, Ihnen sein neues Fahrrad zu zeigen!

Exercise 13 (*b*)

Some possible answers:

1. Man spielt Fussball auf einem grossen Feld hinter der Schule. 2. In einem Wald kann man Nüsse (nuts) und bunte Blätter suchen. 3. Der Junge steckt die Hand in die Tasche und zieht einen Schlüssel hervor (takes out). 4. Auf den Tisch stellt die Frau zwei Teller. 5. Ich muss meine Schwester fragen, wo sie heute abend tanzen will.

Have a Try 13

Good morning, Mrs. Schulze. What can I get you?
Good morning. I'd like a pair of brown shoes.
Oh yes, I remember what size you take. Try this pair, please—they're made of very good, best quality leather.
I'm afraid they're too tight for me. Have you something cheaper?
Will you please try on this pair at 65 marks.

These are quite comfortable. I'll take them.

Thank you very much. Is there anything else?

Yes, a tin of shoe-polish, please.

That comes to 66 marks 20 pfennigs, please. Thanks very much.

Good day! (Good bye!)

Exercise 14 (a)

1. When my hair is too long, I go to the hairdresser. 2. Although it's raining today, I'm not wearing a cap. 3. I come home at half past four. 4. This train leaves at quarter to two. 5. Before the train leaves I buy my ticket.

6. Während ich im Dorf bin, besuche ich meine Grossmutter. 7. Weil ich früh aufstehe, gehe ich früh zu Bett. 8. So oft ich Fussball spiele, nehme ich ein Bad. 9. Wenn der Gottesdienst zu Ende ist, komme ich aus der Kirche. 10. Bis der Arzt meinen Namen ruft, sitze ich im Wartezimmer.

Exercise 14 (b)

fünfundzwanzig Minuten nach fünf; zwanzig Minuten vor zwölf; fünf Minuten nach zehn; Viertel nach sechs; acht Uhr; zehn Minuten nach eins; halb drei; halb sieben; Viertel vor vier; neun Uhr.

Exercise 14 (c)

1. Wenn wir Gemüse brauchen, gehen wir auf den Markt. 2. Um halb acht kommt der Briefträger. 3. Während der Arzt sein Frühstück isst, liest er die Zeitung. 4. Ehe der Zug den Bahnhof erreicht, fährt er über eine Brücke. 5. Obgleich Hans vierzehn Jahre alt ist, ist er doch (= "nevertheless") sehr klein.

Have a Try 14

Krankenhaus, Pantoffel, Geschenke, Schlagball, Fleisch, wiehert, ein Musikinstrument, Geld, eine Kaffeekanne, kalt.

Exercise 15 (a)

1. Wenn ich schnell fahren will, muss ich ein gutes Fahrrad haben. 2. Ehe ich meine Mahlzeit essen darf, muss ich mir die Hände waschen. 3. Weil ich einen neuen Tennisschläger kaufen will, muss ich mein Geld sparen.

4. Obgleich mein Bruder (omit das) Klavier spielen kann, singt er nicht gern. 5. Während meine Frau (sich) das Fernsehprogramm ansieht, kann sie stricken. 6. Weil der Zug abfahren will, steigen die Fahrgäste in die Wagen (Abteile) ein. 7. Wir gehen in den Obstgarten, um Äpfel zu pflücken. 8. Sie brauchen keinen teuren Apparat, um gute Aufnahmen zu machen. 9. Meine Schwester holt ein Messer, um das Brot zu schneiden. 10. Ich knipse das Radio an, um die Nachrichten zu hören.

Exercise 15 (b)

1. Auf dem Bahnsteig will (werde) ich einen Freund meines Bruders treffen. 2. Um sieben Uhr rasselt mein Wecker, um mich aus dem Bett zu treiben. 3. Im Juni können wir im Garten den Duft der bunten Blumen riechen. 4. Die Kinder jener kleinen Schule laufen um vier Uhr aus den Klassenzimmern. 5. Zeigen Sie dem Arzt die wunde Stelle am Kopf!

6. Ein Fahrgast löst seine Fahrkarte, ehe er auf den Bahnsteig geht. 7. Im September findet der Gärtner einen reifen Apfel unter dem Baum.

(Suggested answers): 8. Ein Pferd ist ein Tier, das einen Wagen zieht. 9. Der Schnee fällt im Winter (im Januar). 10. Die Schere liegt im Nähkasten meiner Mutter.

Have a Try 15

A young composer is visiting the great conductor Furtwängler at his villa (week-end residence). "I would like to play you two movements from my new suite 'The Lonely Ones' and hear your opinion of it (them)."

While the composer is playing, Furtwängler sits by the piano to make the acquaintance of the "Lonely Ones". Twenty minutes later the composer turns to Furtwängler and says, "That was one movement from my suite. What do you think of it, maestro?" "I prefer the other," says Furtwängler drily.

Exercise 16 (a)

1. Dienstag, den vierten März. 2. Sonntag, den siebenundzwanzigsten Juni. 3. London, den zehnten Dezember neunzehnhundertdreiundsechzig. 4. Den dritten November neunzehnhunderteinundfünfzig. 5. Am fünften November. 6. Am ersten Mai. 7. Mittwoch, den zwölften Juli. 8. Samstag (Sonnabend), den sechzehnten April. 9. Bonn, den siebzehnten August achtzehnhundertzweiundsiebzig. 10. Am zweiten Februar.

Exercise 16 (b)

1. I mustn't forget to go to the hairdresser('s) at four o'clock.

2. In the café a woman is asking the waiter to bring her an ice.

3. This old postman is trying to read the address without (his) glasses.

4. In October the leaves begin to cover the ground.

5. The boxer is leaving the ring without shaking hands with his opponent.

6. Vergessen Sie nicht, die Tür der Garage zu schliessen!

7. Wir müssen versuchen, den Gipfel des Hügels vor Mittag zu erreichen.

8. Können Sie diese Aufgabe schreiben, ohne ein Wörterbuch zu benutzen?

9. Erwin bittet seinen Vater, ihm ein neues Fahrrad zu kaufen.

10. Mein Wecker beginnt, um Viertel nach sieben zu rasseln.

Have a Try 16

Suppe	*Fischgericht*	*Fleischgericht*	*Nachtisch*
Erbsensuppe	Hering	Schinken	Erdbeereis
Tomatensuppe	Hecht	Leberwurst	Ananas
Kraftbrühe	Forelle	Hühnerbraten	Obst
Gemüsesuppe	Garnelen	Bratwürstchen	Apfelmus
Pilzsuppe	Karpfen	Kalbfleisch	Pfirsiche
Fleischbrühe	Ölsardinen	Wiener Schnitzel	Schokoladentorte
Schildkrötensuppe	Rheinsalm	Hammelfleisch	Käse

Exercise 17 (a)

1. Der Tischler sucht seinen Hammer. 2. Sehen Sie nicht so überrascht aus! 3. Wenn Sie durch das Fenster blicken, können Sie Autos auf der Strasse sehen. 4. Heute abend möchte ich mir ein gutes Fernsehprogramm ansehen. 5. Mütter pflegen ihre Kinder. 6. Plötzlich öffnet sich eine Tür im Raumschiff.

7. The thick woods stretch as far as the sea. 8. When we cross the road, we must always keep a good look-out. 9. In the park an old gardener is bending over a gay flower-bed. 10. In November I feel so comfortable in my warm bed. 11. Look at this beautiful stamp. 12. The green curtain is moving in the wind.

Exercise 17 (b)

Am Morgen stehe ich um sieben Uhr auf. Dann gehe ich in das Badezimmer, um mich zu waschen. Ich muss mich anziehen, ehe ich mein Frühstück esse. In der Küche sitzt meine Frau schon an dem langen Tisch und trinkt eine Tasse Kaffee. Wenn ich fertig bin, suche ich meine Handschuhe.

Endlich öffne ich die Tür der Garage, um mein altes Fahrrad zu holen.

Have a Try 17

A famous professor in Berlin is spending an evening at a friend's house. When he is about to return home it is raining hard. Then his friend's wife asks him to spend the night at their house, because it is still raining so hard. The professor thanks her and says: "I'll be very pleased to stay overnight."

Suddenly the guest disappears. They are just about to go to bed, when the professor comes back into the room, absolutely wet through. "But for goodness' sake," says his friend, "weren't you going to stay the night here, in order not to get wet?" "Certainly," answers the professor, "but I had to dash home to fetch my nightshirt!"

Exercise 18 (a)

1. Kennen Sie einen guten Zahnarzt? 2. Der Pfarrer weiss, was der Organist am Sonntag spielen will. 3. Diese Touristen möchten wissen, ob sie in der Kirche Aufnahmen machen dürfen. 4. Wir essen immer in diesem Hotel, weil meine Familie den Kellner kennt. 5. Fragen Sie jenen Polizisten; vielleicht wird er wissen, wo die berühmte Brücke liegt. 6. Wissen (denn) die Fahrgäste, dass dieser Zug am Sonnabend fünf Minuten früher abfährt?

7. Every child knows that a mountain is higher than a hill. 8. A plane travels faster than a train. 9. My bed is more comfortable than this chair. 10. A pencil is not as useful as a ball-point pen.

Exercise 18 (b)

1. Ein reifer Apfel ist süsser als ein grüner Apfel. 2. Ein scharfes Taschenmesser ist besser als ein stumpfes Taschen-

messer. 3. Ein neuer Teppich ist weicher als ein alter Teppich. 4. Ein Hund ist nicht so gross (stark) wie ein Pferd. 5. Eine Stadt hat mehr Häuser als ein Dorf. 6. Ein Café ist kleiner (billiger) als ein Hotel. 7. Elektrisches Licht ist heller als Gaslicht. 8. Dieser Wecker ist zuverlässiger als meine Uhr. 9. Dieses Buch ist nicht so dick wie ein Wörterbuch. 10. London ist grösser als Berlin. 11. Eine Meile ist länger als ein Kilometer. 12. Jenes Mädchen ist nicht so hübsch wie ihre Schwester.

Have a Try 18

On a dark evening three students are on a journey to Bonn. Suddenly they come to a cross-roads and don't know (now) whether to go to the right or to the left.

Soon one of the students discovers a signpost with three arms. But because it is so dark, none of them can read what is on it. So the first (student) climbs on to the shoulders of the second and strikes a match, but the wind immediately blows it out. Then his friend tries to read the letters, but he has no better luck.

Finally the third student climbs up, breaks off the three arms and jumps to the ground again. Now they can read the word ("inscription") "Bonn" all right, but nobody knows which way it should point!

Exercise 19 (a)

1. Ein Pferd ist ein Tier, das einen Wagen zieht.

2. Aus ihrem Nähkasten holt meine Frau die Schere, die stumpf ist. (or: Meine Frau holt die Schere, die stumpf ist, aus ihrem Nähkasten.) (or: Die Schere, die ... holt, ist stumpf.)

3. Ich habe ein schönes Auto, das schnell auf der Autobahn fährt.

4. Der Kühlschrank, der neu ist, steht in unserer Küche. (or: , der in unserer Küche steht, ist neu.)

5. Ich möchte das Fahrrad, das 100 Mark kostet, mit meinem Taschengeld kaufen.

6. Der Mann, der uns unsere Fahrkarten im Autobus gibt, heisst der Schaffner.

7. Reichen Sie mir bitte das Glas, das auf dem Büfett steht!

8. Ein Messer, das zu scharf ist, kann gefährlich sein.

9. Ein Tischler ist ein Mann, der Tische und Stühle macht.

10. Der Junge, der nebenan wohnt, versucht, ein Modellflugzeug zu machen.

Exercise 19 (b)

1. Wenn der alte Professor zu Bett geht, vergisst er, seine Schuhe auszuziehen. 2. Sie dürfen nicht versuchen, in einen Autobus einzusteigen, wenn er sich (schon) bewegt (in Bewegung ist). 3. Das Feuer beginnt eben aufzuflammen. 4. Ich gehe in mein Schlafzimmer, um mich anzuziehen. 5. Bitten Sie Erich, das Radio anzuknipsen!

(Possible answers): 6. Ein Fahrgast ist ein Mann (Mensch), der mit dem Autobus oder dem Zug fährt. 7. Ein Matrose ist ein Mann, der auf einem Schiff (zur See) arbeitet (fährt). 8. Ein Wecker ist eine Uhr, die mich am Morgen weckt. 9. Im Garten liegt ein Hund, der am Abend in der Küche schläft. 10. Ich muss die Milch trinken, die meine Schwester in das (dieses) Glas giesst.

Have a Try 19

In Germany nearly every town has a theatre. Big cities have an opera-house too, where operas are produced. When we enter the theatre we leave our overcoats, hats or umbrellas in the cloak-room and then go into the auditorium. In front of us is the stage, where the actors appear. We have seats in the stalls; above us are the boxes and circles. When everything is ready, they have to raise the curtain, which is let down again after each act. We buy a programme and wait for the performance to begin.

Exercise 20 (a)

1. Das Haus, in dem ich wohne, hat sieben Zimmer.
2. Der Tisch, an dem ich sitze, steht in der Mitte des Zimmers. (*or:* Ich sitze an dem Tisch, der in der Mitte des Zimmers steht.)
3. Der Zug, auf den ich jetzt warte, fährt um halb zwei ab. (*or:* Ich warte jetzt auf den Zug, der um halb zwei abfährt.)
4. Auf dem Zaun sitzt ein brauner Vogel, den ich füttere.
5. Ich suche meine Füllfeder, mit der ich einen Brief schreiben will.
6. Das kleine Loch, aus dem die Maus kommt, ist neben der Tür. (*or:* Die Maus kommt aus einem kleinen Loch, das neben der Tür ist.)

7. Is your friend interested in stamps? 8. This girl isn't afraid of a little mouse. 9. In the wardrobe, which stands in the hall (vestibule), my old coat is hanging. 10. In the bucket which I see in the kitchen is some dirty water. 11. This morning we are having to wait a long time for the postman. 12. I'm always thinking of the shopping that I have to do in town on Monday.

Exercise 20 (b)

1. Ich warte nicht gern auf mein Frühstück. 2. Kennen Sie den Pfarrer, der am Sonntag in unserer Kirche predigt? 3. Der Duft der Blumen, die meine Mutter pflückt, ist sehr stark. 4. Ich kenne keinen Arzt, der berühmter als Doktor Weiss ist. 5. Jeder Organist muss sich für Musik interessieren. 6. Wie heisst jenes Lied, das Sie singen? 7. Der Kaffee, den wir trinken, ist fast kalt.

8. Der Zug, auf den ich warte, kommt in zehn Minuten an.
9. Das Pferd, das auf diesem Feld arbeitet, sieht müde aus.
10. Das grosse Gebäude, vor dem das Auto steht, (ist das Postamt).

11. Ich habe einen guten Schläger, mit dem ich (Kricket spielen kann).

12. Aus dem Briefkasten, der (an der Ecke der Strasse steht, nimmt ein Briefträger die Briefe).

Have a Try 20

We live in the city centre on the edge of the park, which surrounds the inner part of the town. I would like especially to give you a short description of our "palm garden". Between lawns and flowerbeds are the greenhouses. In the tropical atmosphere thrive rare African plants and flowers, which give out a strange sweet scent. Water-lilies and water-weeds flower on goldfish-ponds. Carnivorous plants, too, are to be seen there. I suppose the nicest thing is the Palm House. Huge palms rise from the beds, where a babbling stream winds, until it eventually ends in a waterfall.

Exercise 21 (a)

1. Have you seen the film which is showing this week at our cinema? 2. I must hear the new radio that my friend has bought today. 3. Ask the porter where he has left the big trunk. 4. I have looked everywhere for my ticket. 5. Where is the magazine that I have been reading in bed? ("have been reading" = "have read"). 6. What has Mrs. Smith given her daughter for her birthday?

7. Karl hat mir ein schönes Bild gezeigt, das er in einem alten Buch gefunden hat. 8. In der Küche hat die Putzfrau ihren Eimer geleert. 9. Das Kind hat die Milch getrunken, die seine Mutter in ein Glas gegossen hat. 10. Hans hat sein Geld gespart, um einen neuen Kugelschreiber zu kaufen.

Exercise 21 (b)

1. Haben Sie je mit jenem Mädchen getanzt? 2. Meine Frau hat einen grünen Pullover gestrickt. 3. Nächste Woche

möchte ich Ihre Schwester treffen. 4. Jeden Morgen schlafe ich bis sieben Uhr. 5. Nächstes Jahr fahren wir nach Frankfurt, wo mein Onkel ein Haus gekauft hat. 6. Nachdem ich mich abgetrocknet habe, will ich ein neues Hemd anziehen. 7. Jeden Abend kommt mein Freund um halb sieben nach Hause. 8. Haben Sie eine Briefmarke auf diesen Umschlag geklebt? 9. Was hat Ihre Schwester in jenem Laden gekauft? 10. Nie hat mein Hund eine Katze gejagt.

Have a Try 21

1. Das Echo. 2. Eine Landstrasse. 3. Die Nase ("nose"). 4. Der Kaffee; er kann sich setzen, der Tee muss ziehen. (sich setzen means to "sit down" *and* "to settle", ziehen means to "pull" *and* to "brew".) 5. Die Sonne ("sun").

Exercise 22 (*a*)

1. Dieser Zug ist von Köln nach Frankfurt gefahren. 2. Ist mein Bruder schon aufgestanden? 3. Hat der Metzger das Stück Rindfleisch verkauft, das ich im Laden gesehen habe? 4. Ein schwarzer Vogel ist über unser Haus geflogen. 5. Die Maus ist in ihr Loch gelaufen, weil unsere Katze vom Stuhl gesprungen ist.

6. Renate is the nicest girl I have ever danced with. 7. I have often tried to climb over this wall. 8. Who has sent you that long letter? 9. When the gardener has dug over the flower-beds, he will gather the last roses. 10. Although the red car has disappeared round the corner, I can still hear it.

Exercise 22 (*b*)

1. Ein Apfel ist von dem Baum gefallen, unter dem Herr Braun sitzt. 2. Zwei Vögel sind aus dem Baum geflogen, weil Herr Braun von seinem Liegestuhl aufgestanden ist. 3. Ist der Zug aus Hamburg angekommen? Ich habe versprochen, meine Schwester an der Sperre abzuholen. 4. Der Arzt wohnt

in dem grössten Haus im Dorf. 5. Ich habe am längsten gewartet. 6. Dieses Licht scheint am hellsten. 7. Obgleich Karl der kleinste Junge in der Klasse ist, hat er (doch) den besten Aufsatz geschrieben.

8. Haben Sie meine Mütze gesehen? Ich habe sie überall gesucht. 9. Nachdem wir die Einkäufe gemacht haben, können wir eine Weile im Park sitzen. 10. Heute hat meine Schwester im Salon Klavier gespielt. 11. Jener Pfarrer hat mit dem Arzt gesprochen. 12. Ist eine Luftreise gefährlicher als eine Reise mit dem Zug?

Have a Try 22

Near Frankfurt is the beautiful and well-wooded Taunus, perhaps the finest mountain range in Germany and a favourite place for the people of Frankfurt to visit. Well-kept paths take visitors to the nicest viewpoints. On almost every individual summit are hotels or vantage-points, which afford a magnificent view of the plain far below.

The highest mountain in the Taunus is the Great Feldberg, 2889 ft. high. Here you get the finest view in the whole of the Taunus. The Feldberg forms a plateau, on which there are three hotels and an observation-post.

The next highest mountain in the Taunus is the Altkönig. Then comes the Little Feldberg, on which stands an observatory for seismological measurements.

Exercise 23 (a)

1. I have no hope of making a space-flight next year. 2. A piercing (cutting) wind is driving the leaves into the street. 3. In that house I can hear a child singing. 4. The ringing of my alarm-clock is very loud this morning. 5. A sleeping dog is lying on my bed. 6. On Sunday we shall have the pleasure of going for a trip into the country. 7. I have read a nice story in the magazine today.

8. Was stecken Sie in die Tasche? 9. Haben die Fahrgäste gefragt, auf welchem Bahnsteig der Zug abfährt? 10. Darf ich das Vergnügen haben, mit Ihrer Schwester zu tanzen? 11. Sehen Sie das Feuer aufflammen? 12. Der Polizist steigt in ein wartendes Auto ein. 13. Ich höre gern das Zwitschern der Vögel in meinem Garten. 14. Weil ich keinen Schlüssel habe, kann ich diese Tür nicht öffnen.

Exercise 23 (*b*)

Es ist Sonnabend. Um Viertel nach sieben steige ich aus dem Bett. Nachdem ich mein Frühstück gegessen habe, muss ich den Brief von Onkel Heinrich beantworten. Dann muss ich zwei Paar Schuhe vom Schuster abholen. Während ich in der Stadt bin, möchte ich die neue Ausstellung moderner Fernsehapparate neben dem Rathaus besuchen. Vielleicht werde ich das Vergnügen haben, Freunde zu treffen und mit ihnen eine Tasse Kaffee im Café zu trinken. Ehe ich wieder nach Haus komme, muss ich am Bahnhof die Züge für unseren Ausflug am Sonntag ausfindig machen.

Have a Try 23

We have been at the sea-side for a fortnight now and we are enjoying it very much. On the very first morning we got up early to see (lit. "experience") a sunrise over the sea. The sun rises like a ball of fire from the water which lies glittering before us.

Wind, sea and sunshine tempt us out of doors every day. I do a lot of swimming, whilst Gisela prefers to occupy herself on the sand(s) or in the beach "basket".* We have had some marvellous walks over the sands; we have also had a good look round a liner.

* A kind of portable wicker-work shelter popular on northern beaches.

Exercise 24 (a)

1. Ich möchte gern die Uhr haben (kaufen), die ich im Schaufenster gesehen habe. (*or:* Darf ich Sie bitten, mir die Uhr zu zeigen, die im Schaufenster ist?)

2. Können Sie mir bitte sagen, wie ich zum Bahnhof komme?

3. Stört es Sie, wenn ich das Fenster offen habe?

4. Können Sie mir bitte sagen, wann das Konzert beginnt?

5. Würden Sie so freundlich sein, diesen Hundertmarkschein zu wechseln?

6. Ich möchte gern zwei Apfelsinen haben.

7. Stört es Sie, wenn ich das Radio anknipse? 8. Können Sie mir bitte sagen, wo die Haltestelle ist? 9. Würden Sie so freundlich sein, mir diese Anzeige zu erklären? 10. Darf ich Sie bitten, langsamer zu sprechen?

Exercise 24 (b)

1. Er *hat* gehalten, gesungen, gelesen, gesprochen, getrieben, gefangen, zerbrochen, gebracht, gerochen, gesehen.

Er *ist* gestiegen, gewachsen, gekrochen, gegangen, gekommen.

2. Can you please tell me how much these brown shoes cost (are)?

3. Would you be good enough to pass me the bread?

4. Because there is no school today, the boys have gone off into the country, singing.

5. Barking, my little dog comes leaping (bounding) into the room.

6. Können Sie mir bitte sagen, in welcher Richtung der Grosse Feldberg liegt?

7. Würden Sie so freundlich sein, die Butter aus dem Kühlschrank zu holen?

8. Stört es Sie, wenn ich im nächsten Zimmer Klavier spiele?

9. Ich habe eine schöne Briefmarke auf diesen Brief geklebt.

10. Ein Fahrgast darf nicht vergessen, seine Fahrkarte vor der Reise zu lösen.

Have a Try 24

"Get up, Tony!" Smiling sympathetically, the mother bends over the sleeping boy. She runs her hand over his brown hair.

"Get up, Tony. It's time!" The old pendulum-clock strikes six, sluggishly (lit. "hesitating") and out of tune. Mother has gone into the kitchen again. Tony begins to get dressed, shivering. A thousand ideas buzz through his head. Then he too goes into the kitchen to wash himself. Mother has warmed the water today. And later, whilst he is sipping the hot coffee, he doesn't see his mother wipe a big shining tear from her eyes. Today the boy is going to the factory for the first time. And her big, affectionate ("loving") heart resists the idea.

Exercise 25 (a)

1. Zwei Männer sitzen in einem Boot, das den Fluss heraufkommt.

2. Die Katze Ihres Nachbars ist in unserem Garten den Pfad hinuntergelaufen.

3. Ein grosses Auto fährt schnell die Strasse entlang.

4. Wenn ich die Küchentür (die Tür der Küche) öffne, läuft mein Hund in den Garten hinaus.

5. Während wir neben der Brücke angeln, klettern die Kinder langsam den Hügel hinauf.

6. Dieser alte Fahrgast, dessen Koffer sehr schwer ist, sucht einen Gepäckträger.

7. Ich verbringe eine Woche bei meiner Tante, in deren Obstgarten ich Äpfel pflücken darf.

8. Der Organist spielt in einer Kirche, deren Turm höher als die Häuser ist.

9. Ich sehe einen Vogel, dessen Nest unter dem Dach des Hauses liegt.

10. Hans hat eine Schwester, deren Taschentuch in die Tinte gefallen ist.

(Other conclusions will do, with *verb last*.)

Exercise 25 (b)

1. My grandfather, whose pipe has fallen on to the carpet, has gone to sleep in his comfortable deckchair. 2. A lot of children come running along the woodland path. 3. In order to look for his ball Erich climbs up on to the garage roof. 4. The children are playing in the wood. Suddenly Robert jumps out from behind a big tree. 5. A gardener, whose wheelbarrow is standing outside the window, has been digging our garden today. 6. In(to) whose desk have you put my ruler?

Have a Try 25

Ein alter Brunnen plätschert mitten auf dem Dorfplatz.
Viele Fahrgäste steigen an der Endstation ein.
Eine lästige Fliege fällt in die Milch.
Der junge Matrose erzählt lustige Geschichten.
Unser Garten sieht im Juli schön aus.
Ein müder Gärtner ruht sich gern in der Mittagspause aus.

Exercise 26 (a)

1. Hast du ein Löschblatt in deinem Pult? 2. Gib dem Lehrer deinen Aufsatz! 3. Vergiss nicht, dass du heute abend zum Friseur gehen musst! 4. Darf ich dich bitten, mir deine Pass zu zeigen? 5. Pass auf! Hinter dir steht ein knurriger Hund.

6. I would like to see what you have in your pocket. 7. (Just) let me see how you write the address. 8. Because you are the strongest, you are to carry the trunk. 9. Are you still there, Jack? Your friends want to talk to you. 10. (Do) come in! We have been waiting a long time for you.

Exercise 26 (b)

1. In this little village water is fetched from an old well. 2. The bucket was emptied by the charlady. 3. Yesterday a lot

of money was offered to us. 4. Stories are often told by sailors.
5. These children's essays are very nicely written. 6. Last week
my old grandmother was taken to hospital.

7. Heute morgen sind die Dächer der Häuser mit Schnee
bedeckt. 8. Fleisch wird beim Metzger gekauft. 9. Sprich
nicht so laut! Dein Bruder ist schon zu Bett gegangen. 10.
Warum willst du dein Frühstück nicht essen? 11. Nachdem
du dich angezogen hast, geh(e) die Treppe hinunter! 12.
Fürchtest du dich (hast du Angst) vor einer kleinen Maus?

Have a Try 26

On Monday morning North Japan was shaken by a severe
earthquake. Near the town of Miyagi a woman was killed by
a falling wall.

On Tuesday the new Teachers' Training College in Langenthal was opened.

On Sagenmatt Street in Lucerne masses of rock have crashed
down and caused serious damage. Fortunately no one was
injured. A dog was rescued alive from the rubble.

Exercise 27 (a)

1. Der Junge steckte etwas in seine Tasche, als ich die Tür
öffnete. 2. Das Mädchen, mit dem ich tanzte, hatte braune
Haare. 3. Meine Frau strickte, während sie (sich) das Radio
anhörte. 4. Das Licht in meinem Schlafzimmer war nicht sehr
hell. 5. Viele Touristen lösten Fahrkarten am Bahnhof. 6.
Nachdem der Tischler sich gewaschen hatte, trocknete er
sich mit einem weissen Handtuch ab. 7. Wir wohnten in
einem grösseren Haus. 8. Obgleich wir so lange im Warenhaus
waren, hatten wir (doch) nichts gekauft. 9. Mein Bruder lachte,
als ich ihm das Bild zeigte. 10. Obgleich ich meinen Hund
gefüttert hatte, war er noch hungrig.

Exercise 27 (b)

1. While I was waiting in the car, my sister was shopping in the town. 2. I was surprised when my alarm-clock rang at half past five today. 3. The child hurt itself, although the toy was not dangerous. 4. In summer we often used to ramble over the hills. 5. The waiter handed me a glass of wine which I had ordered in the café. 6. My dog had soon chased the black cat out of the garden. 7. I was waiting at the hospital when a doctor suddenly opened the door. 8. When I was (still) small, I often used to play with my sister's doll. 9. The parson gave his son a new bicycle as a present. 10. The girl was afraid of the big horse.

Have a Try 27

verlassen, deserted
erleuchtet, lit up
sinnen, to think
die Gasse, the narrow street
schmücken, to decorate

das Kindlein, the little child
beglückt, happy
hehr (poetic), sublime
das Schauern, feeling of awe

Exercise 28 (a)

1. Karl *stieg* in den Autobus ein, *weil* er heute nachmittag in die Stadt *fahren wollte.*

2. Hans *fing* den Ball, *den* sein Freund hoch in die Luft *geworfen hatte.*

3. Gerda *stand* am Fenster, *als* ich ins Zimmer *kam.*

4. Ich *konnte* nicht sehr schnell *laufen, weil* der Wind so stark *war.*

5. Die Maus, *die* vor der Katze Angst *hatte, war* in ihr Loch *gekrochen. or: Weil* die Maus vor der Katze Angst *hatte, war* sie in ihr Loch *gekrochen.*

6. Der Professor las eine Zeitschrift, die er am Bahnhof gekauft hatte.

7. Hans wollte noch skilaufen, obgleich er sich am Montag verletzt hatte.

8. Als ich die Tür geschlossen hatte, versuchte der Polizist, sie wieder zu öffnen.

9. Warum ging Robert zu Bett, ehe er seine Milch getrunken hatte?

10. Wir mussten lange warten, bis der Arzt kam.

Exercise 28 (b)

1. We preferred to go by Underground, because so many people were queueing at the bus-stop.

2. After we had cleared the table, the crockery was carried into the kitchen.

3. When the fire-brigade arrived, black smoke was rising up from the roof of the town-hall.

4. An Englishman was asking the shop-girl if she would show him a cheap watch.

5. I haven't found anything better in the whole shop.

6. Hans came quickly down into the village because he could ski well.

7. At half past six the little child had already gone to sleep.

8. Weil ich ein neues Hemd kaufen wollte, musste ich zum Laden gehen.

9. Der Junge hatte Angst, weil er hinter der Kirche etwas Weisses gesehen hatte.

10. Hans durfte bis halb elf aufbleiben, weil sein Onkel uns besuchte.

Have a Try 28

Franz Ahlmeyer had spent the evening with some friends and was now returning home very late. When he was going along Castle Street, he suddenly saw a man lying on the pavement. He bent over him in surprise and tried to rouse him. But then he saw that he had blood on his hands (lit. fingers). It was obvious that the poor fellow was dead.

While he was still wondering what to do two policemen

came along. As soon as they caught sight of the dead man, they arrested Franz and took him to the police-station, where he was thoroughly questioned. He said, "I know absolutely nothing about the matter," but they refused to believe him.

To his family's horror he was immediately sent to prison, although he knew that he was innocent.

Exercise 29 (a)

the typewriter, the suspension-bridge, the smoke-cloud, the mountaineer, the wallet, the forefinger, the city, the sleeping-car, the toothbrush, the parachute, the puppet-show, the pedestrian, the neighbourhood, the disc (record), the flywheel.

ein Apfelbaum, ein Wasserkrug, eine Haarbürste, Tanz-musik, eine Seereise, Schreibpapier, ein Brotmesser, eine Mädchenschule, Eingang, ein Regenschirm, ein Klassen-zimmer, die Gartenmauer.

Exercise 29 (b)

1. Do you happen to (perhaps) know a good doctor about here? Certainly. The famous Dr. Cranach lives in the first building just round the corner. 2. This scarf is a bit too expensive for me. Have you something similar at three marks? Unfortunately not. 3. Did you take some photos when we were visiting Thorstein Castle? Of course. We're expecting them to turn out very well. 4. We're going (to go) to the theatre tonight. I hope you haven't forgotten to see about the tickets? 5. May I offer you a cigar, or perhaps you don't smoke? Oh yes! I like smoking very much.

6. Ich möchte zwei Plätze für heute abend. Wieviel kosten diese hier in der zweiten Reihe? 7. Es freut mich sehr, dass Sie sich so gut amüsiert haben (dass du dich so gut amüsiert hast). 8. Können Sie mir bitte diesen Fünfzigmarkschein wechseln? Gewiss; kommen Sie (treten Sie) bitte an die

Kasse. 9. Sie dürfen nicht in den Zug einsteigen, weil Sie nur eine Bahnsteigkarte haben. 10. Bitte, wieviel kostet es nach Heidelberg? Fünf Mark? Also gut, zwei Fahrkarten zweiter Klasse bitte, hin und zurück.

Have a Try 29

The day of departure had come. We had been busy packing for a long time the previous evening, for we had to get up very early. After breakfast our friends accompanied us to the station and made sure that we got the right train and some good seats.

We were very pleased with our stay in Germany. During the last fortnight we had had all sorts of excursions, and everywhere the people had been friendly and kind. We were also pretty fluent in German by now. These certainly were the happiest holidays we had ever had.

Exercise 30 (a)

1. Let's run down the hill. There are no trees in our way. 2. During the winter we can often ski across the fields. 3. The higher we climb, the colder the air becomes. 4. Outside the girls' school an old mistress is going for a short walk. 5. A dictionary would be useful if you wanted to give me a present. 6. Hardly had we done the shopping when black clouds began to collect in the sky. 7. It has given us much pleasure to spend the evening with you. 8. Instead of a cap, this policeman is wearing a helmet. 9. Some tourists who arrived yesterday are going for a trip to the next village this morning. 10. I would never have believed it (that).

Exercise 30 (b)

1. Es gibt Leute, die Kricket nie gespielt haben. 2. Es waren einige Äpfel unter den Bäumen im Obstgarten. 3. Ich

möchte meiner Grossmutter einige Blumen schicken. 4.
Warten Sie bitte draussen! Es sind schon zu viele Leute im
Zimmer. 5. Je bequemer mein Bett ist, desto länger schlafe
ich. 6. Kaum waren die Fahrgäste in den Autobus eingestiegen,
als der Schaffner ihnen befahl, wieder auszusteigen. 7. Es ist
sehr kalt draussen. Geben wir den Vögeln etwas Brot! 8.
Kaum hatten wir das Hotel erreicht, als unsere Freunde
ankamen. 9. Jenes Mädchen sieht uns an; machen wir eine
Aufnahme! 10. Während des Abends habe ich zwei Briefe
geschrieben.

Have a Try 30

1. Tyrolese painter.	D efregge R
2. A Sunday in the Church calendar.	Ex au dI
3. Element.	Ra di uM
4. Eastern women's quarters.	Ha r eM
5. Phoenician goddess.	As tar tE
6. Mathematician.	Eu I eR
7. Italian opera composer.	LeoncavallO
8. Opera by d'Albert.	Tief lanD
9. Wavy line.	Ser pentinE
10. Mountain in the Bernese Oberland.	Ei g eR
11. Peninsula in the Adriatic.	Is tri eN (Istria)
12. Finnish sportsman.	Nu r mI
13. Movable rails (points).	Wei chE
14. Night-bird.	Ohr eulE (horned owl)
15. Mountain mass near Lake of Lucerne.	Ri gI
16. Swiss canton.	Tes siN
17. Tributary of the River Bug.	Na reW
18. Insult.	In ju riE
19. Opera by Bizet.	Car meN
20. Constituent of beer.	Hop feN (hops)
21. Map maker (drawer).	To pograpH

22. Character in a Saint-Saëns
       opera.   De   li   lA
23. Strong drug preparation.   Ex   tra   kT

Der haelt (= hält) sein Wort nicht, der immer oder nie ein
"Wenn" hat.

"A man who always (or never!) says 'If . . .' will not keep
his word."

ALPHABETICAL WORD LIST

(Some words are purposely omitted from this general list: they include numbers, days, months, some verbs and prepositions, which are best learnt in their individual Lists in the various Lessons.)

A

der Abend, evening
das Abendessen, supper
aber, but
abfahren, to depart, set off
abholen (W), to go to meet, collect
abräumen (W), to clear (tables)
das Abteil, compartment
abtrocknen (sich) (W), to dry
ach! Oh!
ähnlich, similar
allerlei, all kinds of
alt, old
amüsieren (sich) (W), to have a good time
anbieten, to offer
angeln (W), to fish
anhören (W), to listen to
anknipsen (W), to switch on
ankommen, to arrive
ansehen, to look at
die Anzeige, notice
anziehen (sich), to get dressed
der Apfel, apple
die Apfelsine, orange
der Arzt, doctor
aufbleiben, to stay up
aufflammen (W), to blaze up
die Aufgabe, exercise
aufgehen, to rise (sun, etc.)
die Aufnahme, photograph
aufpassen (W), to look out
der Aufsatz, essay
aufstehen, to get up
ausfindig machen, to find out
der Ausflug, trip
aussehen, to look, seem

die Ausstellung, exhibition
ausziehen (sich), to undress
das Auto, car

B

der Badeanzug, bathing costume
das Badezimmer, bathroom
der Bahnhof, station
der Bahnsteig, platform
der Ball, ball
beantworten (W), to answer
befehlen, to order, command
behaglich, comfortable (of persons)
beissen, to bite
bellen (W), to bark
bequem, comfortable (things)
der Berg, mountain
berühmt, famous
besorgen (W), to get, see to
bestellen (W), to order (meals, etc.)
das Bett, bed
die Bewegung, movement
das Bild, picture
ein bisschen, a little, a bit
bitte, please
bitten, to ask
das Blatt, leaf
blau, blue
der Bleistift, pencil
blicken (W), to look
das Blumenbeet, flower-bed
die Blumenvase, flower vase
brauchen (W), to need
breit, wide
der Brief, letter
der Briefkasten, letter-box

die Briefmarke, stamp
der Briefträger, postman
die Brille, pair of spectacles
bringen, to bring (or take)
das Brot, bread
die Brücke, bridge
der Bruder, brother
der Brunnen, well
das Büfett, sideboard
bunt, brightly coloured
die Bürste, brush
bürsten (W), to brush
die Butter, butter

C

das Café, café

D

das Dach, roof
der Dackel, dachshund
denken, to think
deren, dessen, whose
Deutsch, German (language)
Deutschland, Germany
dicht, thick, dense
dies(er, -e, etc.), this
dort, there
draussen, outside
der Duft, scent

E

eben, just
die Ecke, corner
das Ei, egg
der Eimer, bucket
Einkäufe (pl.), purchases, shopping
einschlafen, to go to sleep
einsteigen, to get in (vehicles)
der Eintritt, entry, admission
elektrisch, electric
emporsteigen, to rise up
der Engländer, Englishman
entzückend, delightful

erklären (W), to explain
erreichen (W), to reach (places)
erzählen (W), to tell (stories)
essen, to eat
etwas, something, some

F

fahren, to travel, go (by bus, etc.)
der Fahrgast, passenger
die Fahrkarte, ticket
die Fahrt, journey
fallen, to fall
die Familie, family
der Farbstift, crayon
fast, nearly, almost
das Feld, field
der Fernsehapparat, television set
das Fernsehprogramm, t.v. programme
fertig, ready, finished
das Feuer, fire
die Feuerwehr, fire brigade
finden, to find
die Flasche, bottle
das Fleisch, meat
fliegen, to fly
das Flugzeug, 'plane
der Fluss, river
der Freund, friend
der Friseur, barber, hairdresser
frisch, fresh
das Frühstück, breakfast
die Füllfeder, fountain pen
fürchten (sich) (W), to be afraid
der Fuss, foot
füttern (W), to feed (animals, etc.)

G

ganz, whole
der Garten, garden
der Gärtner, gardener
die Garage, garage
der Gasherd, gas-cooker

das Gebäude, building
gefährlich, dangerous
gehen, to go, walk
gelb, yellow
das Geld, money
das Gemüse, vegetable
der Gepäckträger, porter
gerade, just, straight
die Geschichte, story
das Geschirr, crockery
gestern, yesterday
giessen, to pour
der Gipfel, summit
glauben (W), to believe
der Gottesdienst, church service
der Grad, degree
gross, big
die Grossmutter, grandmother
der Grossvater, grandfather
grün, green
gründlich, thoroughly

H

das Haar (usually pl. Haare), hair
haben, to have
das Halstuch, scarf
halten, to hold, stop
die Haltestelle, bus stop
der Hammer, hammer
hämmern (W), to hammer
das Handtuch, towel
hängen, to hang
das Haus, house
der Hausflur, hall, vestibule
das Haustier, domestic animal
heissen, to be called
hell, bright
der Helm, helmet
das Hemd, shirt
hier, here
der Himmel, sky
hin und zurück, there and back
hoch, high
die Hoffnung, hope
holen (W), to fetch

das Hotel, hotel
hübsch, pretty
der Hund, dog
der Hundertmarkschein, 100
    mark note
hungrig, hungry

I

interessieren (sich) (W), to be
    interested

J

ja, yes
die Jacke, coat, jacket
jagen (W), to chase
das Jahr, year
je, ever (je grösser, the bigger)
jeder, -e, -es, etc., each, every
jener, -e, es, etc., that
jung, young
der Junge, boy

K

kalt, cold
kaputt, broken
die Kasse, cash desk
kaufen (W), to buy
der Kellner, waiter
kennen, to know (be acquainted
    with)
das (der) Kilometer, kilometre
das Kino, cinema
der Kirchturm, church tower
die Klasse, class
das Klavier, piano
kleben (W), to stick
der Kleiderschrank, wardrobe
klein, small, little
klettern (W), to climb
knurrig, growling
der Koffer, trunk
kommen, to come
das Konzert, concert
der Kopf, head

kosten (W), to cost
das Krankenhaus, hospital
(das) Kricket, cricket
kriechen, to creep, crawl
der Krug, jug
die Küche, kitchen
die Küchenuhr, kitchen clock
der Kugelschreiber, ball-point pen
der Kühlschrank, refrigerator
kurz, short

L

lachen (W), to laugh
der Laden, shop
das Land, country
lang, long
lange, for a long time
lassen, to leave, let
laufen, to run
laut, loud
leeren (W), to empty
der Lehrer, master, teacher
die Lehrerin, mistress
leise, quietly
lernen (W), to learn
lesen, to read
die Leute (pl), people
das Licht, light
der Liegestuhl, deck-chair
das Lineal, ruler
das Loch, hole
das Löschblatt, blotting paper
lösen (W), to buy (tickets)

M

das Mädchen, girl
die Mahlzeit, meal
die Mathematik, mathematics
der Matrose, sailor
die Mauer, wall
die Maus, mouse
die Meile, mile
der Metzger, butcher

die Milch, milk
das Mittagessen, lunch, dinner
das Modellflugzeug, model 'plane
modern, modern
morgen, tomorrow
der Morgen, morning
die Mutter, mother
die Mütze, cap

N

der Nachbar, neighbour
die Nähe, vicinity
der Nähkasten, work basket
der Name, name
nass, wet
nebenan, next door
nehmen, to take, pick up
nein, no
das Nest, nest
nett, nice
nichts, nothing
nie, never
noch, still, yet
die Nuss, nut
nützlich, useful

O

der Obstgarten, orchard
offen, open (adj.)
öffnen (W), to open
oft, often
so oft, every time
der Onkel, uncle
der Organist, organist
die Orgel, organ

P

der Pass, passport
der Pfarrer, parson
die Pfeife, pipe
pflegen (W), to look after
der Platz, place (seat)
der Polizist, policeman

(den, dem Polizisten)
die Post, post (office)
praktisch, practical
predigen (W), to preach
das Pult, desk
die Puppe, doll
die Putzfrau, charlady

R

das Radio, wireless (set)
rasseln (W), to rattle, ring (alarm)
das Rathaus, town-hall
rauchen (W), to smoke
das Raumschiff, space ship
regnen (W), to rain
reichen (W), to pass, hand
die Reihe, row
rein, clean
die Reise, journey
riechen, to smell
das Rindfleisch, beef
die Rose, rose
rostig, rusty
rufen, to call, shout
rund, round (adj.)

S

saftig, juicy
sammeln (W), to collect
der Schaffner, conductor (bus)
die Schale, peel
scharf, sharp
scheinen, to shine
schenken (W), to give as a present
die Schere, scissors
schicken (W), to send
der Schirm, screen, protective cover
schlafen, to sleep
schläfrig, sleepy
das Schlafzimmer, bedroom
der Schläger, bat, racket
Schlange stehen, to queue

das Schloss, castle
der Schlüssel, key
der Schnee, snow
schmutzig, dirty
schon, already
schön, beautiful, nice
schreiben, to write
die Schubkarre, wheelbarrow
der Schuh, shoe
die Schulaufgaben (pl), homework
der Schuster, cobbler
schwarz, black
schwer, heavy
die Schwester, sister
schwimmen, to swim
sehen, to see
sehr, very
sein, to be
setzen (sich) (W), to sit down
singen, to sing
skilaufen, to ski
so, so
sofort, immediately
der Sohn, son
der Sommer, summer
die Sonne, sun
sorgen (W), to care, tend
sparen (W), to save (money)
der Spaziergang, walk
das Speiseeis, ice-cream
die Sperre, barrier
spielen (W), to play
das Spielzeug, toy
springen, to jump
der Spülstein, sink
stecken (W), to put (in pockets, etc.)
stehen, to stand
steigen, to climb
die Stelle, place, position
stricken (W), to knit
die Strasse, street
der Stuhl, chair
stumpf, blunt

suchen (W), to look for
süss, sweet

T

der Tag, day
die Tante, aunt
tanzen (W), to dance
die Tasche, pocket
das Taschenmesser, penknife
das Taschentuch, handkerchief
der Tau, dew
der Teller, plate
der Teppich, carpet
teuer, dear, expensive
tief, deep
der Tisch, table
der Tischler, joiner
der Tourist, tourist
tragen, to carry, wear
treffen, to meet
treiben, to drive, impel
trinken, to drink
das Trinkglas, tumbler
die Tür, door

U

überrascht, surprised
die Uhr, clock, watch
umgraben, to dig over
der Umschlag, envelope
und, and
untersuchen (W), to examine

V

der Vater, father
verbringen, to spend time
das Vergnügen, pleasure
verkaufen (W), to sell
die Verkäuferin, sales girl
verlassen, to leave (places)
verletzen (W), to hurt, injure
versprechen, to promise

vielleicht, perhaps
der Vogel, bird
der Vorhang, curtain
vorlesen, to read aloud

W

wachsen, to grow (bigger)
die Wahrheit, truth
der Wald, wood, forest
das Warenhaus, big stores
warten (W), to wait
das Wartezimmer, waiting room
was, what
das Wasser, water
wechseln (W), to change (money,
    etc.)
der Wecker, alarm clock
der Weg, way
weich, soft
der Wein, wine
weiss, white
welcher, -e, -es, etc., which?
wer? who?
werfen, to throw
wie? how?
der Wind, wind
der Winter, winter
wissen, to know (facts)
wo, where
die Woche, week
wohnen (W), to live, dwell
die Wolke, cloud
die Wolle, wool
das Wort, word
das Wörterbuch, dictionary
wund, sore

Z

der Zahn, tooth
der Zahnarzt, dentist
der Zaun, fence
zeigen (W), to show
die Zeitung, newspaper

die Zeitschrift, magazine
zerbrechen, to break
die Zigarre, cigar
das Zimmer, room

zu, to, too
der Zug, train
zuverlässig, reliable
zwitschern (W), to twitter